John le Carré's
The Spy Who Came In From The Cold

Adapted from

methuen | drama

LONDON • NEW YORK • OXFORD • NEW DELHI • SYDNEY

METHUEN DRAMA

Bloomsbury Publishing Plc, 50 Bedford Square, London, WC1B 3DP, UK
Bloomsbury Publishing Inc, 1359 Broadway, New York, NY 10018, USA
Bloomsbury Publishing Ireland, 29 Earlsfort Terrace, Dublin 2, D02 AY28, Ireland

BLOOMSBURY, METHUEN DRAMA and the Methuen
Drama logo are trademarks of Bloomsbury Publishing Plc

First published in Great Britain 2024
New and updated edition published 2025

The Spy Who Came in From the Cold © John le Carré, 1963

Copyright © David Eldridge, 2024, 2025

David Eldridge has asserted his right under the Copyright, Designs and Patents
Act, 1988, to be identified as author of this work.

For legal purposes the Acknowledgements on p. vii constitute an extension
of this copyright page.

Cover design by AKA

All rights reserved. No part of this publication may be: i) reproduced or transmitted in
any form, electronic or mechanical, including photocopying, recording or by means of
any information storage or retrieval system without prior permission in writing from
the publishers; or ii) used or reproduced in any way for the training, development or
operation of artificial intelligence (AI) technologies, including generative
AI technologies. The rights holders expressly reserve this publication from the
text and data mining exception as per Article 4(3) of the Digital Single
Market Directive (EU) 2019/790.

Bloomsbury Publishing Plc does not have any control over, or responsibility for,
any third-party websites referred to or in this book. All internet addresses given in this
book were correct at the time of going to press. The author and publisher regret
any inconvenience caused if addresses have changed or sites have ceased
to exist, but can accept no responsibility for any such changes.

No rights in incidental music or songs contained in the work are hereby granted
and performance rights for any performance/presentation whatsoever
must be obtained from the respective copyright owners.

All rights whatsoever in this play are strictly reserved and application for performance
etc. should be made before rehearsals by professionals and by amateurs
to Independent Talent, 40 Whitfield Street, London, W1T 2RH.
No performance may be given unless a licence has been obtained.

A catalogue record for this book is available from the British Library.

A catalog record for this book is available from the Library of Congress.

ISBN:	PB:	978-1-3506-1830-5
	ePDF:	978-1-3506-1831-2
	eBook:	978-1-3506-1846-6

Series: Modern Plays

Typeset by Westchester Publishing Services
Printed and bound in Great Britain

For product safety related questions contact productsafety@bloomsbury.com.

To find out more about our authors and books visit
www.bloomsbury.com and sign up for our newsletters.

The Ink Factory and Second Half Productions
in association with Nica Burns
present

The Chichester Festival Theatre production of
John le Carré's

The Spy Who Came In From The Cold

Adapted for the stage by **David Eldridge**

Creatives

Adaptor	**David Eldridge**
Director	**Jeremy Herrin**
Production Design	**Max Jones**
Lighting Design	**Azusa Ono**
Composer	**Paul Englishby**
Sound Design	**Elizabeth Purnell**
Casting	**Jessica Ronane CDG CSA**
Voice Coach	**Hazel Holder**
Fight Director	**Sam Lyon-Behan**
Associate Design	**Joe Lichtenstein**
Associate Lighting Design	**Ruth Hall**
Costume Supervisor	**Laura Rushton**
Props Supervisor	**Kate Margretts**
Wigs, Hair and Makeup Supervisor	**Sharon Pearson**
Casting Associate	**Abby Galvin**
Casting Assistants	**Poppy Apter, Annafrancesca Ottila Boffa**

Production Team

Company Stage Manager	**Francesca Finney**
Deputy Stage Manager	**Anna Townley**
Assistant Stage Manager	**Flynn White**
Head of Wardrobe	**Inmaculada Cook**
Head of Wigs, Hair and Makeup	**Hannah Sinclair**
Deputy Head of Wardrobe	**Emily Souch**
Production Manager	**Kate West**
Associate Production Manager	**Charlotte Ranson**

For The Spy Who Came In From The Cold

General Management	**Second Half Productions**
Marketing Consultant	**Stacy Coyne Wright**
Marketing	**AKA and EMG**

Cast

Alec Leamas	**Rory Keenan**
Liz Gold	**Agnes O'Casey**
Pitt / Ford / Governor	**David Rubin**
Mundt	**Gunnar Cauthery**
Control	**Ian Drysdale**
George Smiley / Karden	**John Ramm**
Karl Riemeck / Kiever / Probation Officer	**Mat Betteridge**
Miss Crail / President of the Tribunal	**Norma Atallah**
Fiedler	**Philip Arditti**
Ashe	**Tom Kanji**
Understudy	**Harriet Leitch**
Understudy	**Martin South**
Understudy	**Matthew Seager**
Understudy	**Nigel Allen**

DAVID ELDRIDGE Adaptor

David Eldridge is an award-winning playwright and screenwriter. His work is performed across the UK and internationally in translation.

His original plays include three plays in a trilogy for the National Theatre, *Beginning, Middle* and *End*; *Market Boy* (National Theatre); *Holy Warriors* (Shakespeare's Globe); *In Basildon, Incomplete and Random Acts of Kindness* (Royal Court) and *Under the Blue Sky* (Royal Court & Duke of York's Theatre, West End: *Time Out* Live and Theatregoers' Choice Awards for Best New Play); *The Stock Da'wa* and *Falling* (Hampstead Theatre); *The Knot of the Heart* (Almeida Theatre: Off West End Award for Best Play); *A Thousand Stars Explode in the Sky* (co-written with Simon Stephens and Robert Holman, Lyric Hammersmith); *Something, Someone, Somewhere* (Sixty Six Books, Bush Theatre); *M.A.D.* and *Serving It Up* (Bush Theatre); *Summer Begins* (Donmar Warehouse); *A Week with Tony*, *Fighting for Breath* (Finborough Theatre); *Dirty* (Theatre Royal Stratford East); *Cabbage for Tea, Tea, Tea!* (Platform 4, Exeter).

Adaptations include new versions of Strindberg's *Miss Julie* and Ibsen's *The Lady from the Sea* (Royal Exchange, Manchester), *John Gabriel Borkman* and *The Wild Duck* (Donmar Warehouse); Jean-Marie Besset's *Babylone* (Belgrade Theatre, Coventry); and *Festen* from the Dogme 95 Film (Almeida, Lyric Theatre West End & Broadway: Theatregoers' Choice Award for Best New Play).

Screenplays include *The Scandalous Lady W* (BBC2), *Our Hidden Lives and Killers* (BBC4) and his many plays for radio include *The Picture Man*, which won the Prix Europa for Best European Radio Drama.

In 2007 the University of Exeter conferred on David Eldridge an Honorary Doctorate of Letters recognising his achievement as a playwright. He is a Senior Lecturer in Creative Writing at Birkbeck College, University of London. Early in 2026 ITV will broadcast his original four-part drama series, *Betrayal*.

PRODUCERS Second Half Productions

Second Half Productions is an entertainment company founded in 2020 by Jeremy Herrin, Alan Stacey and Rob O'Rahilly to generate innovative productions for the stage. By commissioning world-leading artists to create new work and by breathing new life into classic stories, we invigorate audiences in London, the UK and beyond.

Recent and upcoming productions include *Every Brilliant Thing* (Broadway, West End, Edinburgh Festival Fringe), *The Spy Who Came In From The Cold* (West End, UK tour, Chichester Festival Theatre), *Grace Pervades* (Theatre Royal Haymarket, Theatre Royal Bath) *The Little Foxes* (Young Vic), *People, Places & Things* (Trafalgar Theatre), *Long Day's Journey Into Night* (Wyndham's Theatre), *A Mirror* (Almeida, Trafalgar Theatre), *Ulster American* (Riverside Studios), *Best of Enemies* (Noël Coward Theatre), *The Glass Menagerie* (Duke of York's Theatre).

Our team is co-founders and directors, Jeremy Herrin, Alan Stacey and Rob O'Rahilly; Creative Director, Lucie Lovatt; Executive Producer, Alecia Marshall; Casting Director, Jessica Ronane CDG; General Manager, Grace Nelder; Finance Manager, Sophie Wells; Production and Executive Assistant, Immie Maclean; Press and Publicity is by Kate Hassell for Bread and Butter, and Marketing and Sales by Stacy Coyne Wright.

The Ink Factory

The Ink Factory is an independent studio with global reach, founded in 2010 by Stephen and Simon Cornwell.

A core pillar of the company is the adaptation of the work of author John le Carré for film, television and other media.

The Ink Factory's le Carré adaptations include 'The Pigeon Tunnel', directed by Errol Morris, 'The Little Drummer Girl', directed by Park Chan-wook; the Emmy® and Golden Globe® award-winning drama series 'The Night Manager', directed by Susanne Bier; and the Anton Corbijn-directed *A Most Wanted Man* starring Philip Seymour Hoffmann (in partnership with Amusement Park). The company's ground-breaking Hindi-language adaptation of 'The Night Manager' has become Disney+ Hotstar's most watched drama in history. The company is also developing a series based on le Carré's books featuring George Smiley, a contemporary series adaptations of *The Constant Gardener* (in English) and two versions of *A Most Wanted Man* (in German and Korean).

Beyond its le Carré adaptations, the company has worked with filmmakers ranging from Ang Lee, with *Billy Lynn's Long Halftime Walk*, to Stephen Merchant, on his feature directorial debut *Fighting with My Family*. Chadwick Boseman starred in the company's *Message From The King*, co-written by Ink Factory founder Stephen Cornwell, and Jodie Foster led a remarkable ensemble cast in The Ink Factory's dystopian action feature *Hotel Artemis*.

The company is headquartered in London and Los Angeles.

Chichester Festival Theatre

Chichester Festival Theatre creates inspiring experiences that bring people together – on and off the stage. Creativity is at the heart of everything we do, and we aim to light a spark in everyone who experiences our work – locally, regionally, nationally and internationally.

As one of the UK's flagship theatres, we are renowned for the exceptionally high standard of our productions and our industry-leading work with the community and young people. At the heart of our work are our core values: we are creatively ambitious, community-driven, inclusivity champions, and sustainably minded.

The Festival Theatre's bold thrust stage design makes it one of England's most striking playhouses – equally suited to epic drama and musicals. The studio theatre, the Minerva, is particularly noted for premieres of new work alongside intimate revivals. Our new third venue, The Nest, opened in summer 2025: a vibrant space for dynamic work and the talent of tomorrow.

Countless productions which started life at CFT have transferred to the West End or toured nationally and internationally over the past six decades, from musicals to significant new plays and classic revivals. We are thrilled that our production of *The Spy Who Came In From The Cold,* which enjoyed a sell-out run in the Minerva Theatre as part of our Festival 2024 season, is now reaching London and will also tour the UK next year.

We will always aspire to excellence; boldly push boundaries; seek and support current and future voices; and ensure everyone feels that they belong.

To read more about us, visit cft.org.uk.

John le Carré's
The Spy Who Came In From The Cold

Adapted from the novel by David Eldridge

Leamas
Smiley
Control
Karl Riemeck
Pitt
Miss Crail
Liz
Ford
The Prison Governor
The Probation Officer
Ashe
Kiever
Fiedler
Mundt
The President Of The Tribunal Judges
Karden
Shoppers, Officers of the Abteilung, Prisoners, Guards and Soldiers.

Parts should be doubled as each production sees fit, with the exception of Smiley and Karden, who should be played by the same actor.

The presence of the Berlin Wall is felt throughout.

For David Cornwell

Scene One

Leamas *alone, watching with binoculars.*

Leamas The year is nineteen-sixty-one. October, to be precise. Germany is a country split in two. A kind of uneasy hell. Like two brothers taught to hate each other. On one side is the Soviet Union and their allies in the communist east. And on the other side is good old Uncle Sam and his allies in the west. One night in August a wall is erected in Berlin by the GDR. To stop their people leaving for the west. The city is divided, an open wound. A place of brinkmanship, scheming, and machination. A place where one balls up could turn a cold war hot. A place for the dirty business of spying.

Mundt *enters.*

Leamas This is Mundt. My sworn enemy. The Head of the Abteilung. The intelligence service of East Germany. Tonight my agent's coming over and if there's one bastard who'll get in the way it's bound to be Mundt. You know before the war he was a Nazi. And now he's a communist. How times change.

Control *enters.*

Leamas This is Control. The Chief. He's in charge of the British Secret Intelligence Service and its Headquarters on Cambridge Circus. And I'm his man in Berlin. Head of the Berlin Station. And if it was up to me we'd have brought my agent over a year ago. But Control wanted to bleed him dry.

Karl Riemeck *enters wheeling his bike.*

Leamas And this, this is Karl. My agent. Member of the East German Secretariat and the Praesidium. British Spy. The Crown Jewels. He gave us everything we wished for and more. The best agent I ever had. But it's come to an end and it's time for Karl to join his friends in the West. And live a quiet, ordinary life. Where are you, Karl, damn you?

Control Agents aren't aeroplanes, Alec. They don't have schedules.

Leamas Get out of my head, Control.

Control Mundt's after him and he's only got one chance.

Leamas I need to concentrate.

Mundt Bad luck Leamas.

Leamas You as well, damn you.

Suddenly there's light and noise. Soldiers appear, kneel and aim their rifles at **Karl Riemeck**. **Karl** *gets on his bike and starts to pedal furiously.* **Leamas** *turns, panicking.*

Shots ring out. **Karl Riemeck** *topples over with his bicycle, dead.*

Leamas Karl! Karl!

Leamas *wants to go to* **Karl** *but* **Control** *restrains him.*

Leamas You bastard, Mundt! You fucking bastard! He was all I had left. He was my friend!

Control *and* **Mundt** *melt away.*

Leamas And who am I? I'm Alec Leamas. The Spy Who Came in from the Cold.

Scene Two

Leamas *and* **Control**.

Control Tell me Leamas, are you tired of spying? You must be awfully tired. Do you find it cold in here?

Leamas No, not especially.

Control *offers* **Leamas** *a cigarette. He takes it, lights up and smokes.*

Control You're going to find these more expensive.

Leamas Karl Riemeck's dead.

Leamas *looks at* **Karl Riemeck***, who walks through with his bicycle.*

Control It's very unfortunate.

Leamas It is.

Control I suppose that woman of his blew his cover?

Leamas Hmm.

Control Karl's mistress.

Leamas I suppose it was pillow talk.

Control And Mundt had him shot.

Leamas It was bound to be his woman that blew his cover. Bloody fool.

Control How did you feel?

Leamas How did I feel?

Control When Riemeck was shot.

Leamas Hmm.

Control You saw it, didn't you?

Leamas I was bloody annoyed.

Control Surely you felt more than that?

Leamas I was annoyed.

Control Surely you were upset?

Leamas Well.

Control That would be more natural.

Leamas More natural?

Control Yes.

Leamas I was upset.

Control Of course.

Leamas Who wouldn't be?

Control Did you like Karl?

Leamas What do you mean?

Control Did you like him?

Leamas In what sense?

Control As a man.

Leamas I suppose so.

Control You suppose so?

Leamas Yes.

Control Would you say you were friends?

Leamas I went carefully with him after he told me about his mistress.

Silence.

Control You saw Karl shot?

Leamas Yes.

Control What happened?

Leamas His bicycle made this bloody awful racket. It was dark. But there was blood.

Control How did you spend the night?

Leamas What night?

Control What was left of it?

Leamas When?

Control After Karl had been shot.

Leamas There doesn't seem much point in going into it.

Control Tell me.

Leamas Look, what is this? What are you getting at?

Control Would you like a glass of water?

Leamas No.

Control Perhaps something stronger?

Leamas No, thank you.

Control You look upset.

Leamas I'm fine.

Control You look angry.

Leamas I'm absolutely fine.

Control You look like you would like to strangle me. I didn't realise you were so attached to Karl.

Leamas I said no such thing.

Silence.

Control What a dismal failure Berlin's been lately. Karl Riemeck was the last, wasn't he? The last of our people in the East. All of them eliminated by Mundt. But Karl was a man you knew and liked. A foolish man, yes. But your friend. And certainly not the first man undone by a woman.

Leamas I dare say.

Control You were like a father, a brother. He shared with you his deepest fears and insecurities and you reassured him. You fed him, looked after him, kept him safe from harm. Yes he was working for the Circus and being paid handsomely for it. But the relationships we have with our agents are rarely restricted only to the business of spying. For a time he was yours. And you were his. And then you saw him shot and killed.

Leamas He's not the first man I've seen shot and killed.

Control I wondered if you'd had enough?

Leamas What do you mean enough?

Control I wondered whether you were tired.

Leamas Of course I'm tired.

Control Whether you were too upset about Karl Riemeck to go on? Do you want to come in from the cold? I don't want to pry but now you have returned from Berlin. I wondered if you would see your wife and your children?

Leamas No.

Control You don't want to see your children?

Leamas They barely know me.

Control I wondered if you'd visit your father.

Leamas I've not been over there for years. And I've no intention of going back.

Control I wondered whether you were rather feeling alone.

Silence.

We have to live without sympathy, don't we? That's impossible. Of course. One can't be out in the cold all the time.

Leamas I can't talk like this, Control. What do you want me to do?

Control I want you to stay out in the cold a little longer. You could do one last thing for The Circus.

Silence.

Control The ethic of our work is based on a single assumption. We are never going to be aggressors. Do you think that's fair?

Leamas *nods.*

Control We're defensive in the main. I think that's still fair. But we do disagreeable things. So that ordinary people can sleep safely in their beds at night. And on occasion we do very wicked things. I would say that since the war, our methods and those of the opposition have become much the same. How can one be less ruthless than the enemy simply because your government's policy is benevolent? That would never do.

Leamas Yes.

Control What can you tell me about Mundt?

Leamas He's a cold bastard.

Control Yes. Go on.

Leamas Hans-Dieter Mundt's childhood is enigmatic. But we know he was indoctrinated into the Hitler Youth before the war and served in the Waffen-SS. He survived the occupation and he returned to the East and was recruited into the Abteilung. Earlier in his career he was in London. An Intelligence Officer operating under the cover of the East German Steel Mission. Codename 'Blondie'. Mundt was given all the dirty business. Harassment of the Worker State's political enemies. Blackmail, roughing them up. He'd no compunction about killing. Didn't mind it one bit. Murdered an F.O. Man and tried to make it look like suicide. He tried to kill George Smiley, didn't he?

Smiley *appears,* **Leamas** *notices him.*

Control You know about that?

Leamas Yes.

Control I didn't realise you and Smiley were so familiar?

Leamas We're not. I haven't seen him in years. But he's one of a handful in the game worth anything. I wish we were more familiar. He's a damn sight more use than the Cavalry Boys who treat The Circus as if it's no more than a Regimental Club. I was glad to be posted to Berlin and bloody well out of it.

Control I see.

Leamas Smiley was looking into a car he suspected Mundt of using near the Battersea General Hospital and he didn't see the bastard approach him from behind.

Focusing on **Smiley**.

Leamas He struck the blow with a cosh of some kind and he fractured your skull, didn't he George?

Control But Mundt didn't succeed and we may be thankful for that.

Leamas After two days in hiding unfortunately he eluded the grasp of The Circus and got on a flight out of London Airport. Since his return to the East his rise to becoming the Head of the Abteilung has been surprisingly swift. No doubt promotion after promotion reward for killing all my agents. You know, he likes to kill those he regards as traitors himself.

Control Mundt likes to kill them himself does he?

Leamas He likes to drown them. With his own bare hands.

Control Tell me, are you tired of spying? Forgive me if I repeat the question. Do say if you are.

Silence.

I think we ought to try and get rid of Mundt.

Leamas Get rid of Mundt?

Control Yes. I think we should try and get rid of Mundt.

Leamas *laughs*.

Leamas So how the hell do you expect to do that?

Control What I have in mind is a little out of the ordinary. Tell me, do you drink a lot?

Leamas What do you mean?

Scene Two

Control Whisky and that sort of thing?

Leamas I drink a bit.

Control A bit?

Leamas More than most I suppose.

Control You ought to ferret George Smiley out. I'm sure he'd be more than delighted to assist.

Leamas *looks at* **Smiley**.

Leamas What are you doing now George?

Smiley Smiley will do.

Control Smiley's on sabbatical and who knows if he will come back? He's doing things on seventeenth-century Germany. Trouble is, Smiley was never quite able to decide if he wanted to be a spy or an Oxford Don.

Leamas Where is he?

Control He lives in Chelsea. Behind Sloane Square.

Leamas Hmm.

Control Bywater Street. Do you know it?

Leamas Yes.

Control He knows what I have in mind.

Leamas Does he?

Leamas *looks at* **Smiley**.

Leamas Do you?

Control I'm sure Smiley would like nothing more than to get his own back on Mundt.

Leamas I'm sure he would.

Control I think you might make a lot of money out of it. You can keep whatever you make.

Leamas Thanks.

Control That is, of course, if you're sure you want to.

Leamas Yes, I'd like to.

Control Good. Good.

Leamas Nothing would give me greater satisfaction. Than permanently resolving the problem Mundt poses. But I can't see how it could be done, Control.

Control You say you drink more than most?

Leamas Yes.

Control Good. Very good. You'll be very convincing in the role I'd like you to play.

Leamas Go on.

Control I know it's crass. 'Poor Alec Leamas' nothing left in Berlin. He's come back to London full of anguish after witnessing his best agent killed. Drinking far too much to dull the pain. You know, Alec?

If you should meet any old friends at The Circus I should be rather short with them. Let them think we've treated you badly. You know the kind of chap I mean. A resentful kind of inebriated bore.

Leamas Yes, I see.

Control You'll see out the last few months of your contract in the Banking Section. There are some errands to run for me. Some hopping on and off of aeroplanes. Making certain deposits abroad. Helsinki, Copenhagen, Oslo. You know the sort of thing?

Leamas I do. To what end?

Control Framing Mundt as a British spy.

Leamas Well that certainly has a certain appeal.

Leamas *laughs*.

Control The Operation to get Mundt has been well prepared. We'll leave the details for now but when Hans

Dieter Mundt withdraws the money in those banks in Helsinki, Copenhagen and Oslo he won't be aware that money was deposited by you on behalf of The Circus. And his fate will be sealed. By the time you've completed the remainder of the operation he'll be tried as a traitor to the Worker State. An enemy of the people, condemned to make the acquaintance of Frau Guillotine.

Leamas I see.

Control We weren't sure of our man. Who at The Circus has the right qualities to pull it off? Then tragically Karl was killed and you've come in from the cold.

Leamas Yes. I see.

Control The tongues will wag. 'Poor Alec Leamas. A little too fond of a drop of whiskey now.' Then Alec Leamas leaves without warning one day. Your colleagues will rue how far you've fallen. 'Alec Leamas was a hero of occupied Holland during the war. One of the SOE's best men in his day.'

Smiley The SOE's only real success story in the Netherlands. One of the very few agents parachuted in there to survive the war. How did you do it?

Leamas I operated alone and refused to work with the Dutch Resistance. It was all a cock up from beginning to end. I wasn't going to go down with them.

Smiley Very good, Alec. Intelligence work has one moral law. It is justified by results.

Smiley *melts away.*

Control East German intelligence will take notice and perceive you as vulnerable as you drift from taking one crummy dead-end job to another.

Leamas You want me to organise all that myself?

Control One must not break the spell. Then the Abteilung will try to recruit you. And then you will be set.

Leamas I understand what you want.

Control You mustn't feel you have to do it.

Silence.

In our world we pass so quickly out of the register of hate or love. And all that's left in the end is a kind of nausea. You never want to cause suffering again.

They tell me after Karl Riemeck was shot you walked all night. Walked through the streets of Berlin. Is that right?

Leamas Yes, I went for a walk.

Silence.

Control Tell me, Leamas, are you tired of spying?

Leamas Listen. If it's a question of killing Mundt, I'm game.

Scene Three

Leamas *and* **Pitt**. **Pitt** *reads* **Leamas**'s *reference.*

Pitt Mr Leamas, you've been dismissed from two jobs within the space of a month. I'm afraid your reference is rather inadequate.

Leamas I can't say I'm surprised.

Pitt It rather limits your opportunities. Why did you leave a good job like that?

Leamas The Post Room at the Foreign Office isn't at the summit of my ambitions in life.

Pitt Have you taken a drink this morning, Mr Leamas?

Leamas Of course I bloody haven't. How dare you.

Pitt So you were subsequently employed as a Personnel Officer at an adhesive manufacturers?

Scene Three

Leamas At a glue factory, yes.

Pitt And you left that employment after a week? What was the matter there?

Leamas It took a fortnight to rid my clothes and hair of the stench of the glue.

Pitt Tell me why were you dismissed from your recent employment?

Leamas It's none of your bloody business.

Pitt Mr Leamas you're being bloody difficult.

Leamas No matter how many grey streets I trudged up and down there were never enough suburban housewives who wanted to purchase an encyclopaedia.

Pitt So you were a failure at the job?

Leamas I accidentally lost the encyclopaedias.

Pitt Accidentally lost?

Leamas I daresay they found a good home when they were eventually discovered in the Memorial Park, in Pinner.

Pitt You reside in Bayswater?

Leamas Yes, I live in a flat there.

Pitt Do you have access to running hot water in your flat?

Leamas I do for a shilling.

Pitt Then I suggest Mr Leamas you clean yourself up. As it happens you may be in luck. I may have something very convenient for you.

Leamas I see.

Pitt It's not really your cup of tea.

Leamas I dare say. What is it?

Pitt But the pay's fair.

Leamas I see.

Pitt And the work is easy for an educated man.

Leamas For God's sake man, what is it?

Pitt A library.

Leamas A library?

Pitt Yes.

Leamas What sort of library?

Pitt It's the Bayswater Library for Psychical Research.

Leamas The Bayswater Library for Psychical Research?

Pitt Yes. It's an endowment.

Leamas A library for crackpots who believe in ghosts?

Pitt They're an odd lot.

Leamas I dare say you think I'll fit right in.

Pitt I think you may. I think you may.

Leamas I see.

Pitt They want another helper. I'm afraid one can't rely on Unemployment Benefit in perpetuity, Mr Leamas. Beggars cannot be choosers. I'm afraid you'll have to take the job in the library.

Leamas *examines him, thinks.*

Leamas You're very familiar.

Pitt I beg your pardon?

Leamas They way you say 'I think you may'. 'I think you may.' I'm sure I recognise you.

Pitt Well I can't think where from?

Leamas What did you do in the war?

Pitt I'm afraid that's none of your business.

Leamas *notices* **Karl** *wheeling his bike.*

Scene Four

Leamas *notices* **Miss Crail** *waiting*.

Leamas I'm the new help.

Miss Crail Help?

Leamas My name is Leamas.

Miss Crail What do you mean help?

Leamas An assistant. I was sent by the Labour Exchange.

Miss Crail An assistant?

Leamas Yes.

Miss Crail Sent by the Labour Exchange?

Leamas Yes.

He offers his hand but she declines to shake it. So instead he passes her a piece of paper with his particulars.

Miss Crail I know who you are. You live in the Mansions.

Leamas I think you must be mistaken we've not been introduced.

Miss Crail Were you thrown out of The Royal Oak for shouting at a woman?

Leamas I don't recall.

Miss Crail You may address me as Miss Crail.

Leamas Crail, will do. You may address me as Mr Alec Leamas. Esquire.

Miss Crail And the Labour Exchange have sent you?

Leamas A Mr Pitt.

Miss Crail They've not sent anyone else in over a fortnight so I suppose you may as well stay. But I am keeping an eye on you, Leamas. I don't know where you've come from. And I don't much care.

Liz *enters. She's younger than* **Leamas**.

Leamas *is immediately captivated and* **Liz** *is flustered.*
Miss Crail *goes.*

Leamas I'm the new man.

Liz How do you do.

Leamas My name's Leamas.

Liz Pleased to meet you Mr Leamas. I'm Liz Gold.

Leamas *offers his hand.*

Liz Have you met Miss Crail?

Leamas Yes but she's on the phone.

Liz We're marking at the moment.

Leamas I beg your pardon?

Liz Miss Crail's started a new index. It's a question of checking that all the books are on the shelves. Why don't you start on the archaeology? I'll show you how.

Leamas What happens about lunch?

Liz Oh I bring sandwiches.

Leamas Right.

Liz You can share mine. If that would help?

Leamas *shakes his head. They look at each other for as long as you think you can get away with.* **Miss Crail** *comes back in.*

Miss Crail Mr Leamas?

Leamas Leamas. Miss Gold suggested I start on the archaeology.

Miss Crail Use pencil.

Leamas Pencil?

Miss Crail Yes, I will ink in the reference when I have checked.

Leamas I will be going out at lunch time.

Miss Crail I'm afraid you will not.

Leamas I have shopping to do.

Miss Crail No, no, no, shopping is not allowed. We do not allow the bringing of shopping into the library. You will be expected to take a normal lunch break. We do not have time to go shopping.

Leamas Perhaps if we took an extra half an hour for lunch we'd have the time then. And we could work an extra half an hour at the end of the day. If pushed.

Miss Crail *is outraged but decides to respond by shaking her head gravely and going.*

Leamas *looks at* **Liz** *and laughs.* **Liz** *is unsure, but joins in. She likes him. They look at each other.*

Scene Five

Leamas *notices* **Karl** *wheeling his bike towards him.*

Leamas Why are you looking at me like that? You've no right to judge Karl!

Karl *goes.* **Liz** *lights a candle, places it on the floor between them.*

Leamas Thank you for the invitation.

Liz I've been thinking of inviting you since last week.

Leamas Then why didn't you?

Liz I thought you wouldn't come. So I thought I'd simply ask today and see.

Leamas A very cosy set up?

Liz Thank you.

Leamas I don't make a habit of going back to bedsitters. With women I barely know.

Liz I should hope not!

Liz *laughs and* **Leamas** *relaxes, lights up a cigarette.*

Liz Are you married?

Leamas What business is that of yours?

Liz Doesn't a girl want to know what sort of man she's asked to supper?

Leamas Are you married?

Liz Of course I'm not. Do you have any children?

Leamas *smokes, thinks.*

Liz Tell me Alec, what are your interests? What are your beliefs? What do you believe in? What does Alec Leamas believe in?

Leamas *laughs.*

Liz Don't laugh.

Leamas I believe an Eleven Bus will take me to Hammersmith. I don't believe it's driven by Father Christmas.

Liz Seriously, what do you believe in?

Leamas Why do you ask?

Liz Because you're an enigma.

Leamas Is that a compliment?

Liz You must believe in something. I know you do, Alec.

Leamas I'm not sure I do.

Liz You've got that look sometimes.

Leamas A look?

Liz As if you've something special to do.

Leamas Something special? I never knew . . .

Liz Like a priest. Don't laugh . . .

Leamas *laughs.*

Leamas I've been called a few things.

Liz *laughs.*

Leamas I don't like loudmouth Americans bossing everyone around and acting like they own the place. And simply because good old Uncle Sam runs the show now. And I don't like public schoolboys acting like they still run the show. As if the cock-up in Egypt never happened.

Liz You mean Suez?

Leamas Yes I mean Suez. I don't like military parades and people who play at soldiers. People who've never seen the whites of the man's eyes you're about to shoot dead.

Liz What did you do in the war, Alec?

Leamas I don't like to talk about it.

Liz Are you deeply affected?

Leamas No, no, I'm not.

Liz You know we must talk about these things . . .

Leamas I don't like conversations about life either.

Liz Alec –

Leamas And I don't like people who tell me what to think.

Liz Why did you come and work at the library?

Leamas The Labour Exchange put me on to it.

Liz But why?

Leamas I didn't have a job.

Liz What did you do before? Before you were unemployed?

Leamas I don't like to say.

Liz Are you ashamed?

Leamas No.

Liz Were you an undertaker?

Leamas *laughs his head off and shakes his head.*

Leamas No.

Liz Were you involved in criminality? Yes? How exciting. Perhaps, a confidence trickster. Or a brute working for the Maltese in a seedy basement in Soho.

Leamas No.

Liz Miss Crail hates you.

Leamas I know.

Liz She can't abide you.

Leamas I hate her with equal quantities of venom. She deliberately misspells my name. She likes having an enemy. It gives her an excuse to spend half an hour on the telephone to her mother.

Liz How do you know?

Leamas Because I overheard her whispering 'He's the most appalling man, Mother'. There, the clue's in the word 'mother'. I know you're Jewish.

Liz Yes, I am.

Leamas Why've you never mentioned it?

Liz Does it matter?

Leamas Do you go to the synagogue?

Liz No.

Leamas Then what was all that talk about?

Liz You've got me wrong. All wrong.

Leamas What does Liz Gold believe in?

Liz Don't you like the candle light? I do. Are you hungry?

Leamas No.

Liz There's a sadness in you.

Leamas Thanks, I don't need your pity.

Liz And an anger. Where does that come from?

Leamas I should mind your own business if I were you. What do you want with a nobody like me?

Liz A nobody?

Liz *laughs*.

I should rather think you've a high opinion of yourself.

Leamas Hardly.

Liz The sensitivity and confidence. It's something I find rather attractive.

Leamas You'll make me blush.

Liz You know what I believe in? I believe in history.

Leamas History?

Liz Yes.

Leamas Oh Liz, oh no.

Liz What?

Leamas You're not a bloody communist?

Leamas *laughs,* **Liz** *smiles, but blushing, a little hurt.*

Liz Yes, I am. So, what if I am? At least I believe in something. Why should I pay fifty shillings a week to a crummy landlord when we could all own a share in everything? Why shouldn't there be a society where each person contributes? And each person receives according to their needs? I've my whole life in front of me. Why shouldn't we work for a better world?

Leamas Yes.

Liz I believe in all sorts of things. I believe in love. I believe in the liberation of women. I believe women are unsatisfied with the idea that to be considered feminine we must not work. Or be educated. Or have political views. Is that your belief, Alec?

Leamas No, certainly not.

Liz I believe if a woman likes the look of man. She should be free to invite him to her home for a meal. And if they get along. And there's some mutual attraction between them. She should be free to suggest to him, he might like to take her to bed. Without being considered a tart.

Leamas I certainly would not consider you that.

They consider each other.

Liz What is it, Alec, don't you like me?

Leamas *goes to her and they kiss, passionately. Until he breaks it off. She goes for another kiss and he pushes her away.* **Liz** *feels a little hurt. He leaves.*

Scene Six

Liz *and* **Miss Crail**, *looking at her watch.*

Miss Crail I hate to say I told you so. But I knew this would happen, Miss Gold.

Liz I'm sure there must be a good reason why Alec's not here?

Miss Crail We are both well aware of the reason for Leamas's tardiness.

Liz I've no idea what you're getting at, Miss Crail.

Miss Crail Mr Leamas has taken a drink.

Liz No, Alec wouldn't. Not in the morning.

Miss Crail It is half past eleven now and he has had his fair chance.

Liz I know him and this is not like him at all.

Miss Crail You're only a girl. What do you know about his sort?

Liz We're friends and I know something's wrong.

Miss Crail I should be wary of friendship with a man like that.

Liz No, Alec's a good man.

Miss Crail He is a drunk. And I daresay he is a seducer.

Liz Oh Miss Crail, please.

Miss Crail Mrs McCaird agreed to clean for him. Which she didn't have to do. And she said he was downright uncivil. His flat was squalid. And he had no family photographs.

Liz I'm not sure what you're trying to say, Miss Crail.

Miss Crail And she also said he only possessed a few books. One of which she was certain was filthy.

Liz This is nothing but tittle-tattle.

Miss Crail That's as may be. But I'm afraid I am going to telephone the Labour Exchange. I'm afraid they'll have to send a new help. Miss Gold, where are you going?

Liz To the Mansions. That's where he lives, isn't it?

Liz *goes.*

Scene Seven

Leamas *lies down and* **Liz** *brings him a blanket, which she uses to cover him.*

He sleeps. **Liz** *takes out a book which she reads fitfully as he writhes with his fever. She feels his hot head and watches* **Leamas** *calm gradually into a deeper restorative sleep. She kisses him on the forehead.*

Then he wakes. They look at each other. She puts down her book.

Leamas You're here?

Liz Yes.

Leamas Why are you here?

Liz You've been very ill, Alec.

Leamas Have I?

Liz Yes, you were, you were very ill indeed.

Leamas I suppose I was.

Liz I'm afraid a man had to use a hammer to get the lock of your door open. I went to fetch him.

Leamas Oh.

Liz I gave you some aspirin and some beef tea. And you slept. And slept. I was afraid, Alec.

Leamas Afraid of what?

Liz That I'd lose you. I cleaned your flat.

Leamas *sits up with* **Liz**'s *help to look. Silence.*

Liz The fever's gone now.

Leamas I don't remember I . . .

Liz I sat with you. I ran my fingers through your hair.

Leamas Yes . . .

Liz I think the tenderness comforted you.

Leamas Yes, I think I remember now.

Liz I brought some calves-foot jelly.

Leamas Calves-foot jelly? I ate that?

Liz Yes, when you felt like eating.

Leamas The thought of it makes me feel ill.

Liz It's good for you. 'Fisnoga'. It's Ashkenazi. I don't know why but I could see a whole life together. You and I.

Liz *smiles*.

Leamas How long has it been?

Liz Six days.

Leamas That long?

Liz I've come every day.

Leamas Why are you bothered nursing an old man like me?

Liz You know why, Alec.

Leamas I don't.

Liz I can't bear to think of you alone.

Leamas I didn't ask you to come.

Liz But something might have happened to you.

Leamas And I suppose I've to go to the trouble of having the door repaired now?

Liz I'll give you the money . . .

Leamas I don't want your money.

Leamas *stands and* **Liz** *tries to help him but he shrugs her off.*

Leamas Don't follow me again.

Liz How can you say that, Alec?

Leamas I've a job I have to do.

Silence.

You need to leave now.

Liz Is this goodbye?

Leamas Yes it is. Goodbye, Liz. Goodbye.

Liz *is upset and goes.*

Scene Eight

Leamas *and the Grocer,* **Ford**. *He passes* **Leamas** *a carrier bag. A queue has formed.*

Leamas You'd better send me the account.

Ford I'm afraid I can't do that.

Leamas Why the hell not?

Ford I'm afraid I can't give you credit. I don't know you.

Leamas Don't be bloody silly.

Ford I beg your pardon?

Leamas You're Ford. Mr Ford. And I'm Leamas. Mr Alec Leamas.

Ford I don't know any Leamas.

Leamas I've been coming here for months.

Ford We always ask for a banker's reference before giving credit.

Leamas Don't talk bloody cock. Half your customers have never seen the inside of a bank and never bloody will.

Ford I don't know you.

Leamas Don't lie.

Ford And I don't like you.

Leamas I like you even less.

Ford Now sling your hook.

Ford *tries to recover the carrier bag.* **Leamas** *hits him with the side of his left hand and then with the same rapid movement catches him with his elbow.*

He is knocked clean out, his cheek fractured and jaw dislocated. **Leamas** *looks at* **Ford** *and goes.*

Scene Nine

Leamas *and* **Liz** *sit opposite each other. Prison.* **Leamas** *has a letter in his hand.*

Leamas You should never have written to me.

Liz I needed to know how you were.

Leamas All this writing about feelings.

Liz If you didn't want to see me then why did you send me a Visiting Order?

Silence.

Leamas I've something to say to you and I didn't want to put it in a letter.

Liz What do you want to say, Alec?

Leamas You know they open your letters?

Liz Who does?

Leamas The Warders read all the letters. Why should some bloody, grubby Prison Warder know all my business?

Liz I don't care who knows how I feel. It's the truth.

Leamas Keep your voice down.

Liz I don't care what you've done.

Leamas *examines* **Liz**.

Leamas Why do you have to talk like this?

Liz Do you love me, Alec?

Leamas I don't believe in fairy tales.

Liz Alec, tell me, do you love me?

Leamas I shouldn't have asked you to come. Scrubs isn't a place for a girl like you. It was a mistake.

Liz Don't say that, Alec.

Leamas What does it matter whether I love you or not?

Liz We're meant to be together.

Leamas Well you're wrong. You couldn't be more wrong.

Liz I'm not. I know we are. And you know it. The moment we set eyes on each other. It was there.

Leamas *considers her. Silence.*

Liz What's it like in here?

Leamas It's about as rotten as you'd expect.

Liz Do you have friends you can pass the time with?

Leamas *laughs.*

Leamas I make no acquaintances and none are made with me.

Silence.

Scene Nine

Liz And how are you, Liz? What have you been doing to occupy yourself while I've been in here? It must have been a dreadful shock to hear what had happened with Ford and to hear I'd been sent to prison. You must be feeling distressed and confused and hurt?

Leamas I'm sorry.

Liz I'd almost given up. I've been thinking of going away.

Leamas Where?

Liz Bayswater's so drab.

Leamas No.

Liz I had a friend who went to Cuba as part of an "International Work Brigade" trip. He helped build a school. I like the idea of living and working as part of a collective.

Leamas Don't do that.

Liz Why shouldn't I? It's warm. There are good socialists there.

Silence.

Leamas Don't go. Listen to me.

Liz What is it, Alec?

Leamas When I'm released from here I'm going away.

Liz I'll come with you.

Leamas You can't.

Liz Why not?

Leamas Listen to me.

Liz Tell me.

Leamas It might be a month. It might be a year.

Liz Why as long as that?

Leamas I told you, I've a job I have to do. But there's plenty of money to be made. That's all you need to know. And I'll come back. I'll find you.

Liz Will you? Really?

Leamas There might be enough money to buy a house. As long as you've no ideological objection to my owning property?

Liz *laughs.*

Liz What job do you have to do, Alec?

Leamas Isn't what I've said enough for you?

Silence.

Liz I won't go. I'll wait for you.

Leamas Put me out of your mind. Live your life as if you never knew I existed. But know that one day I'll return.

Liz *leans forward and kisses* **Leamas.** *They become aware they're under the scrutiny of a Warder.*

Liz Goodbye, Alec. Don't forget me.

She stands and goes.

Scene Ten

Probation Officer *and the* **Prison Governor** *appear.*
The Probation Officer *gives* **Leamas** *a brown parcel.*

Prison Governor What are you going to do now you're to be released?

Leamas Make a new start.

Prison Governor Excellent. An excellent way to look forwards.

Probation Officer I have the details of an opportunity that may suit?

Leamas Yes?

Probation Officer You could become a male nurse.

Leamas A nurse?

Probation Officer At a mental home in Buckinghamshire.

The Probation Officer *glances at* **The Prison Governor**.

Probation Officer Don't you know, the rail's been electrified as far as Great Missenden.

Leamas Well I'll take that into consideration.

Prison Governor What about your family?

Leamas I don't see them.

Prison Governor Can't you make things up with Mrs Leamas?

Leamas No.

Prison Governor No?

Leamas She's remarried.

Leamas *smiles.* **The Governor** *and* **The Probation Officer** *go.*

Leamas *gathers himself and walks. He's followed by a man,* **Ashe**. **Leamas** *can't bothered to carry his parcel and dumps it.*

Following behind, **Ashe** *picks it up.*

Scene Eleven

Leamas *and* **Ashe** *sit opposite one another. The brown parcel sits between them.*

Leamas Why did you follow me for half an hour?

Ashe I thought you were somebody I once knew in Berlin.

Leamas Hmm.

Ashe I thought you were Alec Leamas. Are you?

Leamas Who the hell are you?

Ashe I'm Ashe.

Leamas Ashe?

Ashe With an E.

Leamas I've no idea who you are.

Ashe I thought you were Alec Leamas. I used to be in the BBC in Berlin. And I borrowed some money from you. I've had a conscience about it ever since. You don't remember me?

Leamas No.

Ashe We met at a party. That Chap from *The Observer* gave it in his flat off Kudamm. All the press boys were there. Surely you remember?

Leamas No.

Ashe He was such a nice man. He gave such lovely pizza parties?

Leamas I've never been to a 'pizza party'.

Ashe We were drinking stingers. Brandy and crème de menthe. And I must say we were all rather tiddly. There were some really gorgeous girls.

Leamas Were there?

Ashe Half the cabaret from the Malkasten. Surely you must remember now?

Leamas It's ringing a bell. What's your name again?

Ashe Ashe. William Ashe. But people call me Bill.

Leamas Bill Ashe?

Ashe Look, this is all rather embarrassing. But we finished up in a night club. With three of the girls. You and I. And a chap from the political adviser's office. And I was so dreadfully embarrassed. Because I hadn't any money on me and you paid. I wanted to take one of the girls home. And you lent me another tenner.

Leamas I lent you another tenner?

Ashe I was ever so grateful. And it had been an age since I had the chance to pop my nuts.

Leamas 'It had been age since I had the chance to pop my nuts?' Christ.

Leamas *thinks and laughs. So does* **Ashe**.

Leamas I remember now. Of course I do.

Scene Twelve

Control *offers* **Leamas** *a cigarette. He lights up.*

Control You're certain no one saw you arrive here?

Leamas No one saw me.

Control You're sure?

Leamas I hopped on and off the bus and the tube before I was driven here.

Control Were you deposited on the King's Road?

Leamas No.

Control On Bywater Street?

Leamas I wasn't seen.

Control How did you find prison?

Leamas It was alright.

Control Was it?

Leamas But the stench.

Control The stench?

Leamas The taste of the place is still coating the roof my mouth.

Control Yes, I see.

Leamas The smell of it's still in my nostrils.

Control The smell of what?

Leamas I'm sure you can use your imagination.

Control Of incarcerated men?

Leamas Disinfectant.

Control Well, I'm sorry we couldn't improve conditions for you.

Leamas Hmm.

Control Provide little extra comforts . . .

Leamas It was alright.

Control But that would never have done.

Leamas Of course not.

Control One must be consistent. At every turn one must be consistent. We mustn't break the spell. You know she's in The Party, don't you?

Leamas Who?

Control Miss Gold. Liz Gold, isn't it? The girl you were involved with before you were sent to prison.

Leamas Yes.

Control I was surprised. Given what happened to Karl Riemeck after he became involved with that woman.

Leamas It was only a fuck.

Control Oh, I see.

Leamas If you know I slept with her a couple of times then I'm sure you're well aware I've not seen her again.

Scene Twelve

Leamas *studies* **Control**.

Leamas I don't want her brought into this.

Control If it was only a fuck why should she be?

Leamas I was only making the point.

Control I see.

Leamas I know how these things go.

Control And how's that?

Leamas All offensive operations take sudden turns in unexpected directions.

Control Quite so.

Leamas You think you've caught one fish and you find you've caught another.

Control A very good analogy, Leamas.

Leamas I want her kept clear of it. Do you understand me, Control?

Control Oh, quite, quite. Quite so. Do you want anything done about her? Money or anything?

Leamas I'll take care of it myself when it's over. Until then I want her left alone. I don't want her to be messed about. I don't want her to have a file or anything. I want her forgotten.

Control I'm sorry, I'm neglecting my duties as deputy host.

Leamas Who was that man in the Labour Exchange?

Control What man?

Leamas Pitt. The man who put me on to 'the Bayswater Library for Pyschical Research'. He was very particular about it.

Control Pitt, you say?

Leamas Wasn't he in The Circus during the war? Is he your man?

Control Of course he's not my man.

Leamas I was sure I recognised him. It was the way he said 'I think you may'. 'I think you may'.

Control I know no one of that name. Pitt, did you say?

Leamas Yes. He was keen I took the job.

Control In the Labour Exchange, you say?

Leamas Oh, for God's sake.

Control Leamas, if I may, I feel you're succumbing to paranoia.

Leamas Am I indeed?

They consider each other. **Leamas** *notices* **Smiley** *appear.*

Leamas Where's Smiley?

Control He's out. He said we could borrow his house. And as you can see it's as ordinary as one would expect a chap like Smiley to own.

Leamas I sent him a card but he didn't reply.

Control Is that so?

Leamas They picked me up this morning. A chap called Ashe. We're meeting again tomorrow.

Control Good, very good.

Leamas Everything is proceeding as planned.

Control Good.

Leamas Odd that the host of the party doesn't want to play?

Control Would you care for a drink?

Leamas   Why isn't George Smiley here?

Control   I was wrong in my assumption. He doesn't like the operation. But he's content for us to meet here. Smiley says he hears you're a good egg and he understands Bywater Street is usefully anonymous. Presumably why he and Ann bought the house in the first place.

Leamas   Does he know the reason for the operation is to try and get Mundt?

Control   Yes.

Leamas   And he still doesn't like it?

Control   It isn't a question of moralities.

Leamas   I'd be surprised if it was. He hates Mundt. Perhaps, even more than I do. It's a great shame if it all works out I won't have the satisfaction of rubbing him out myself.

Control   Smiley's like the surgeon grown tired of blood. He's content that others should operate but he wants no part in it.

Smiley *cleans his glasses.*

Leamas   Hmm.

Control   Mundt's a good intelligence officer and a very hard man. We should never forget that. But we've set the man to trap himself. It's a sly inductive operation.

Leamas   An 'inductive operation'?

Control   Yes.

Leamas   I see. How are you so certain it will get us what we want?

Control   Let's simply say I am.

Leamas   How do you know the East Germans are on to it?

Control That has been taken care of. Everything went off without a hitch in Helsinki and Copenhagen and so on?

Leamas Exactly as planned. I was damned nervous carrying all that money in cash but it was deposited without any questions asked.

Control Very, very, good.

Leamas And you're certain Mundt withdrew all that money?

Control I am.

Leamas But how can you be so sure, Control?

Control When you're approached by whoever's running Ashe they will likely ask you to go overseas. To somewhere you know. They'll do whatever they can to put you at your ease. Where were you deployed in the war?

Leamas In the Netherlands.

Control Yes, I expect they'll take you off somewhere there for the interrogation. The Hague. A couple of weeks should see you through.

Leamas Yes.

Control Always remember to dislike them. Then they will prize what they get out of you.

Leamas I know how to play the game.

Control The ground's prepared. We did it long ago. You're the last stage in the treasure hunt.

Leamas Hmm.

Control Tell them everything you know about Karl. Betray him fully. It doesn't matter now, does it Alec? Let them understand how valuable he was to us.

How prized and important an asset he was to The Circus. How much treasure he provided. Tell them about the

errands you ran for me. Copenhagen. Oslo. Helsinki.
How much money you were depositing. Rely fully on the
resentment you feel towards The Circus. Keep it all as close
to you as possible. Let them draw their own conclusions.

They'll begin to wonder and suspect Mundt. Karl must
have had help, they'll begin to whisper amongst themselves.
Suspicion will inevitably fall upon Mundt. And after that,
the thing should run itself. The worker state will eliminate
Mundt for us.

Leamas They won't take me to the GDR?

Control The GDR?

Leamas They won't take me into East Germany? Once
I'm on the other side of the Wall I'll never be able to get
back over.

Control Why should they take you east? You've only one
story to tell them? Karl.

Leamas *notices* **Karl Riemeck** *walk his bicycle through.*

Control You'll have to lie low while the chemistry works
itself out. But you won't mind that.

Leamas I dare say.

Control We'll make sure you're taken care of. And then you
can find a way to play happy families with your pretty little Jew.

Silence.

Control Oh dear, you've that look again, Leamas. It's
actually what you want isn't it?

Leamas No.

Control No?

Leamas No.

Control Well, one thing I can promise you: it's worth it,
Alec. Eliminate Mundt and we've won a great victory.
Until then, put Liz Gold out of your mind.

Control *goes.* **Leamas** *looks at* **Smiley**.

Leamas Why didn't you reply to the card I sent you?

Smiley I've been busy.

Leamas Are you really working on German literature? Or have you left The Circus to patch things up with your wife?

Smiley Your marriage was hardly perfect, Alec.

Leamas You want to get back at Mundt don't you George.

Smiley I want a quiet life with Ann.

Leamas You know what Philology is, don't you George? It's the study of language. It's development. Literature, writing. The way people talk. The establishment of their authenticity.

Smiley Very good, Alec.

Leamas 'Inductive operation' isn't a term Control would use, would he George?

Smiley It's no longer my concern.

Leamas What's going on? Why weren't you here?

Smiley *melts away.* **Leamas** *thinks.*

Scene Thirteen

Leamas *and* **Ashe**. **Leamas** *drinks whisky and* **Ashe** *pink gin. They're in a strip joint in Soho.* **Smiley** *watches.*

Ashe What do you think?

Leamas I've seen better in Berlin.

Ashe Admittedly I'm not a frequent patron of the Pussywillow Club.

Leamas You astound me.

Ashe Do you want a girl?

Leamas A bottle of Scotch will do.

Leamas *notices* **Liz**.

Leamas I close my eyes for a moment. And we're lying together. My hand falls across your breast. Brushes against your hair. Tucks a strand gently behind your ear . . . What have you done to me Liz? I don't know myself.

Kiever *enters.* **Leamas** *snaps out of it, glances at* **Kiever** *and turns to* **Ashe**. **Liz** *melts away.*

Leamas You didn't tell me we'd be three?

Ashe Leamas, this is Kiever. Kiever, this is Leamas.

Leamas Who's paying for this jolly?

Ashe I am.

Leamas You are?

Ashe I've looked after you up until now, haven't I?

Leamas Yes, you have.

Kiever You run along home. I'll look after this.

Ashe *goes.*

Leamas Perhaps you'll tell me why that man Ashe picked me up?

Kiever I told him to.

Leamas Why?

Kiever I want to make you a proposition.

Leamas A proposition?

Kiever A journalistic proposition.

Leamas A journalistic proposition?

Kiever Yes.

Leamas I see.

Kiever A man with your kind of experience. Of the international scene.

Leamas They'd have to pay a hell of a lot.

Kiever They are offering a downpayment of fifteen thousand pounds.

Leamas That's a lot of money.

Kiever Well – a man of your expertise, shall we say . . .

Leamas And what's the catch?

Kiever My clients reserve the right to put questions to you over the period of one year on payment of another five thousand pounds. But we will travel to The Hague in the morning. A week minimum. But no longer than two weeks.

Leamas I see. How soon do you want an answer?

Kiever Now.

Leamas Now?

Kiever Yes.

Leamas Well I haven't a passport.

Kiever I took the liberty of obtaining a passport for you. We're flying tomorrow morning at nine forty-five.

Leamas *nods and offers his hand. They shake hands.* **Kiever** *goes.*

Scene Fourteen

Leamas They've taken me to Holland. To the Hague.

Smiley As Control suspected they would. Keep calm, Alec.

Leamas *waits on a chair. He is distracted by* **Smiley**.

Smiley You attended the talk I gave at The Circus before the war?

Scene Fourteen

Leamas I remember it as if it were yesterday.

Smiley A man who plays a role, not to others, but alone, is exposed to obvious psychological dangers. The practice of deception is not particularly exacting. It is a matter of experience. Of professional expertise. It is a facility most of us can acquire. But while a confident trickster, an actor or a gambler can return from his performance to his admirers, the secret agent enjoys no such relief.

Leamas They won't take me into East Germany?

Kiever *enters. He has a newspaper.* **Smiley** *melts away.*

Kiever How are you?

Leamas I'm very well.

Kiever You went for a walk this morning? How did you find it?

Leamas Not much had changed.

Kiever Have you been back to the Hague since the war?

Leamas No and I wouldn't have gone out of my way to.

Kiever I read the transcripts of your interviews. Very good. Thank you.

Leamas When am I going back to England?

Kiever I'm afraid you cannot return to England.

Leamas Listen, chum, defection was never on offer . . .

Kiever You cannot stay here.

Leamas Why?

Kiever Your photograph's in the London evening papers.

Kiever *passes* **Leamas** *the newspaper.*

Kiever The British are looking for you.

Leamas No they can't be.

Kiever Or at least they're saying they're looking for you.

Leamas What do you mean by that?

Kiever One must look at all the possibilities in this game, wouldn't you agree Leamas?

Leamas Do you honestly think I wanted to come to The Hague?

Kiever Settle down, Mr Leamas.

Leamas I've done what is necessary. And now I'd like to go home.

Kiever Out of the question.

Leamas Did you do this?

Kiever I'm afraid we'll have to take you East.

Leamas To Germany?

Kiever I don't have that information. But there is no other possibility.

Leamas Give me my money and a passport. I'll look after myself.

Kiever It is decided. Whether you will go to the GDR. I have no answer to give you. That is for my superior to decide.

Leamas You've got me on the fucking hook now, haven't you?

Kiever It is for your own protection.

Leamas Get stuffed.

Kiever Regard it as a visit to the dentist.

Leamas You blew me sky high.

Kiever You may not believe me, but we didn't tell them. We didn't want your people to know.

Leamas I agreed to meet with your man here. A week or two in The Hague. That was our agreement. I made no agreement to go into East Germany.

Kiever Well that is simply a matter of tough luck.

Kiever *goes.* **Leamas** *notices* **Liz** *is there.*

Liz You promised me you'd come back.

Liz *melts away.* **Leamas** *is alone supressing a howl of rage he takes it out on the chair, which he smashes to pieces.*

Scene Fifteen

Leamas *notices* **Smiley** *appear.* **Mundt** *and* **Control** *are there too.* **Karl** *looms with the bike again.*

Leamas Did you do this, Control?

Control Alec.

Leamas *notices* **Mundt**.

Leamas What's he doing here, George?

Smiley *shrugs.*

Leamas Get out of my head! Leave – me – in – peace!

Mundt You're on your own now, Leamas.

Leamas You don't look very menacing do you? He doesn't look very menacing does he?

Mundt I know you are agitated but there is no need to stoop to personal insults.

Leamas How shall I address you?

Mundt However you wish.

Leamas Will 'Blondie' do?

Mundt *laughs, so do* **Control** *and* **Smiley**.

Mundt What is it? You're itching to ask me something? I can see. A little patience, Leamas, and you will soon be in my country and we will meet in a real place. And apart from the frenzy of your racing mind.

Leamas The F.O. man you killed when you were in London?

Mundt Yes.

Leamas He was a Jew wasn't he? And his wife, the one your colleague murdered. She was a Jew.

Mundt Yes.

Leamas You bastard.

Mundt Comrade Mundt and the Worker State know what the Jews deserve.

Leamas I'm going to put an end to you.

Mundt On the contrary, Leamas. I am going to put an end to you.

Mundt *makes to leave*.

Leamas How did you escape from London so easily?

Mundt I assure you it was not easy.

Leamas How?

Mundt Perhaps your so-called Intelligence Services may be more effective if they were run by fewer Old Etonians and puffed-up public schoolboys.

Leamas How did he do it?

Control It's a matter of the greatest regret Mundt escaped our grasp, Leamas.

Leamas I can't go home now, George.

Smiley You always knew it was a possibility . . .

Leamas I thought they'd take me off somewhere but not this . . .

Smiley Surely you realised the terms were too generous?

Leamas Why would I?

Smiley You did not heed the warning . . .

Leamas Was it Control? Was it Control that blew my cover and started the hue and cry?

Smiley Steady yourself, Alec.

Leamas *is distracted as he notices* **Liz**. *He's pleased to see her. He looks around,* **Smiley**, **Control** *and* **Mundt** *all privy to his private thoughts.*

Leamas I had a walk along the beach this morning and I saw a girl with a dog. She had hair and a coat similar to yours. And I noticed myself noticing this thing. And I realised that it is a gift that you have given me . . .

Liz What gift?

Leamas A longing for some kind of normality . . .

Liz Normality?

Leamas An ordinary life.

Mundt *laughs.*

Smiley Did you love her, Alec? Do you love her?

Leamas What does it matter whether I love her? She's gone now.

Smiley I see. Well that is a great pity. A great pity indeed.

Leamas I expect they'll take you off somewhere for the interrogation. It may even be abroad. A couple of weeks should see you through. And after that, the thing should run itself. You'll have to lie low while the chemistry works itself out. But you won't mind that. We'll make sure you're taken care of.

Smiley The operation, Alec. The operation.

Leamas Why are you in my mind? Why are they here?

Smiley Who else do you have?

Smiley You didn't really think Control planned this on his own did you?

Leamas Is it your operation?

Smiley An over-promoted Cavalry Boy quite capable of flirting with Her Majesty. But do you really think Control has a mind capable of conceiving and running an operation such as this?

Control We'll make sure you're taken care of, Leamas.

Leamas It's you, George. Control's simply the front. It's your operation, isn't it George? You liars, both of you, you fucking liars. I can't breathe.

Leamas *barks with anger and frustration.*

Interval.

Scene Sixteen

Leamas *alone.* **Fiedler** *enters.*

Fiedler Welcome to the GDR.

Leamas Up yours. You know damn well I'd never have come to your rotten little half country unless I had to. Your people must be laughing themselves sick.

Fiedler It's unfortunate.

Scene Sixteen

Leamas So you're Fiedler?

Fiedler Yes.

Leamas The Dauphin himself. The pretender to Mundt's throne. I suppose you're after get Mundt's job now.

Fiedler The sooner we're all done, the sooner you can go home.

Leamas You know perfectly well I can't go home. You've seen to that.

Fiedler *pours them both a whisky. Silence.*

Fiedler Do you like water? I ordered soda, but they brought some wretched lemonade.

Leamas Oh, go to hell.

Fiedler Tell me about Karl Riemeck.

Karl Riemeck *appears with his bicycle.*

Leamas I've been through this once already in The Hague.

Fiedler You know the form, Mr Leamas.

Leamas *watches* **Fiedler** *drink. Silence.*

Leamas One day I went for a picnic in the woods on the edge of East Berlin with a colleague and his family. He had a British military number plate on his car. And he parked up beside the canal. After the picnic his children ran on ahead with the basket. And they found somebody had forced the car door. Nothing was stolen. But on the driving seat was a tobacco tin.

Riemeck And in the tin was a small nickel cartridge. The film cartridge of a sub-miniature camera. It contained the minutes of the last meeting of the Praesidium.

Fiedler Yes.

Leamas That's how it started.

Fiedler I see. What was the reaction at The Circus?

Leamas I decided to keep The Circus at arm's length.

Fiedler Why?

Leamas Well I knew I'd hit the gold mine with Karl. And I didn't want to take the risk of the whole damn thing being blown sky high. But I came to an important conclusion quite quickly. The intelligence placed the source in the Praesidium Secretariat. And the Secretariat was very small. And I knew from my work there was a man there called Karl Riemeck.

Fiedler Did all the intelligence you mentioned in The Hague come from Karl Riemeck?

Riemeck Yes it did.

Leamas *looks at* **Karl Riemeck**.

Leamas Why not? You know how much he saw.

Fiedler Did you never have the feeling he got assistance from someone else?

Leamas No. No. It never occurred to me.

Fiedler Did they ever ask where Riemeck got his camera from? Who instructed him in document photography?

Leamas No.

Fiedler Do go on.

Leamas I met him a week later. And we went for a walk.

Fiedler You got a lot out of him?

Leamas It lasted much longer than I expected.

Fiedler When Karl died you flew back to London?

Leamas Yes.

Fiedler Did you remain in London for the rest of your service?

Leamas What was left of it.

Fiedler What job did you have in London?

Leamas Banking Section. Supervision of agents' salaries. Overseas payments for clandestine purposes.

Fiedler You heard about that woman?

Leamas What woman?

Fiedler Karl Riemeck's mistress.

Leamas What of her?

Fiedler She was found dead a month ago. She was shot from a car as she left her flat.

Leamas *looks at* **Karl**.

Fiedler Perhaps she knew more about Karl's network than you did?

Leamas What the hell do you mean?

Fiedler I wonder who killed her?

Leamas *and* **Fiedler** *leave*.

Scene Seventeen

Liz *and* **Smiley**.

Smiley You were friendly with Alec Leamas?

Liz How did you know?

Smiley Did you ever write to him?

Liz No.

Smiley You didn't visit him in prison?

Liz No, I didn't. I was rather preoccupied with the idea of going to Cuba at the time.

Smiley I see. Does anyone else know you were friendly with him?

Liz No.

Smiley Did you go to the trial?

Liz No.

Smiley No press men called?

Liz No.

Smiley Creditors?

Liz No.

Smiley No one at all?

Liz No one else knew.

Smiley Did it surprise you when Leamas beat up Mr Ford?

Liz Of course it did.

Smiley Why do you think he did it?

Liz I don't know. Because Ford wouldn't give him credit, I suppose.

Smiley Do you believe that?

Liz Why shouldn't I believe it?

Smiley Leamas has got two children by his marriage. Did he tell you?

Silence.

Liz I didn't care about his past. I was in love with him.

Smiley Was he in love with you?

Liz I don't know. I don't know if he loved me. He never said.

Smiley Are you still in love with him?

Liz Yes.

Smiley Did he ever say he would come back?

Liz No.

Smiley But he did say goodbye to you?

Silence.

Nothing more can happen to him. I promise you. But we want to help him. And if you have any idea why he hit Ford. If you have the slightest notion then tell us for Alec's sake.

Liz Please go. Please don't ask any more questions.

Smiley *takes a card from his wallet and gives it to* **Liz**. *She looks at it.*

Smiley If you ever want any help. If anything happens about Leamas or . . . Ring me up. Do you understand?

Liz Who are you?

Smiley I'm a friend.

Liz I thought you said you were from the Special Branch?

Smiley One more thing.

Liz Please go now.

Smiley Did Alec know about The Party?

Liz Yes.

Smiley How?

Liz I told him.

Smiley Does The Party know about you and Alec?

Liz I've told you. No one knew.

Smiley You're sure about that?

Liz Where is he? Tell me where he is.

Smiley You did write to him in prison didn't you?

Liz No.

Smiley You know prisoners' letters are read. Especially prisoners of interest like Alec Leamas.

Silence.

Liz Yes, I wrote to him in prison. I said that I'd wait for him always. Why won't you tell me where he is?

Liz *wipes her eyes. Silence.*

Smiley He's gone abroad. We don't quite know where he is. It was a mistake to visit him in prison. It's a great pity. But we'll see you're looked after. For money and that kind of thing.

Liz Who are you?

Smiley A friend of Alec. A good friend.

Scene Eighteen

Leamas *and* **Fiedler**.

Fiedler My dear Leamas, you have presented us with an intriguing problem. You have only given us one piece of intelligence. You told us about Karl. We knew about Karl Riemeck.

Leamas *laughs*.

Fiedler Tell me what you remember about working in the Banking Section at The Circus.

Leamas It was dreary.

Fiedler What bank did you use?

Leamas Blatt and Rodney. A chichi little bank in the City. There's a sort of theory in The Circus that Etonians are discreet.

Fiedler So you knew the names of agents all over the world?

Leamas No, of course I didn't. I got a couple of trips out of it. Dumping money at banks. That was all.

Fiedler Dumping money?

Leamas I went to the Royal Scandinavian Bank in Copenhagen. And the National Bank of Finland in Helsinki. I deposited the money. Ten thousand dollars in Copenhagen. Forty thousand Deutsche Marks in Helsinki.

Fiedler Who for?

Leamas An agent. There was another one in Oslo.

Fiedler Do you know of a reason why payments were made by someone travelling from London?

Leamas Control was running it himself.

Fiedler Control was running it himself?

Leamas Yes. But he used a postman. Me.

Fiedler When did you make your journeys?

Leamas Copenhagen on the fifteenth of November. I flew back the same night. Helsinki at the end of January. I stayed two nights there. Flew back around the twenty-eighth. I had a bit of fun in Helsinki.

Fiedler And the other payments? When were they made?

Leamas I can't remember. Sorry.

Fiedler But one was definitely in Oslo?

Leamas Yes. I can't add to that.

Fiedler These large sums of money deposited in foreign banks. What did you think they were for?

Leamas They were payments to an agent.

Fiedler An agent from behind the Iron Curtain?

Leamas I thought Control had something big. Someone big.

Fiedler Was the alias of the agent you were depositing money for always the same?

Leamas No. I know they had a false passport for identification purposes. But the agent must have travelled on his own passport.

Fiedler The agent travelled on his own passport?

Leamas Yes, I think so.

Fiedler It occurs to me that you could help us to establish whether any of that money was ever drawn.

Leamas You're dreaming . . .

Fiedler If the money has been drawn we shall know where the agent was on a certain day.

Leamas You'll never find him . . .

Fiedler That seems to be a useful thing to know. You could write a letter?

Leamas I never agreed to write letters to banks.

Fiedler The first stage in your interrogation is nearly complete. But the profession of defector demands great patience.

Fiedler *goes to the window.*

Fiedler You should see it here in the autumn. It's magnificent when the beeches are on the turn.

Fiedler *turns back to* **Leamas**.

Leamas You're going to keep me on ice?

Fiedler We can do with you as we please.

Silence.

We have facilities here for people. Facilities for diversion. And so on.

Leamas No, thank you.

Fiedler I make no judgement.

Leamas I don't want a woman.

Fiedler You had a woman in England, didn't you? The girl in the library?

Leamas *explodes*.

Leamas Don't ever mention her again! Or you'll never get another bloody word from me as long as I live! Tell that to Mundt. Or whichever little alley cat told you to say it.

Silence.

Fiedler Did you know Mundt was once in London?

Leamas Yes, I knew.

Fiedler Codename 'Blondie'. Yes? Mundt got about all right. He found it quite easy.

Leamas So I hear. He even managed to kill an F.O. man.

Fiedler So you heard about that too?

Leamas Mundt bloody nearly killed George Smiley as well.

Fiedler It was amazing that Mundt managed to escape at all.

Leamas I suppose it was.

Fiedler You wouldn't think he'd have a chance against the whole of the British security services?

Leamas From what I hear, they weren't too keen to catch him anyway.

Fiedler What did you say?

Leamas I heard The Circus never really wanted to catch Mundt. I never knew quite what happened.

Fiedler British intelligence didn't want to catch Mundt? You are sure of that? No full-scale search?

Leamas Mundt must have been mad. You may well be able to get away with assassination in the Balkans. Or here. But not in London.

Silence.

Fiedler There's one thing that puzzles me. It's odd. It didn't worry me before I met you.

Leamas What's that?

Fiedler Why you ever betrayed your country.

Leamas Money.

Fiedler *thinks.*

Fiedler Why did Mundt have each one of your agents killed? Not one survived. Every person of interest we picked out of the pool. Eliminated. I begged him, 'Why not let me have them for a month or two? What good are they to us when they are dead?'

Silence.

You know what it was? Mundt was afraid. He was afraid we would catch one who would talk too much!

Leamas You're out of your mind.

Fiedler Mundt escaped so easily from England. Was he their man? Did they turn him? Was that the price of his freedom? You provided the answer. You yourself, Leamas. Karl could not have done it all by himself. Karl Riemeck was simply the vessel. It was Mundt all along. Mundt belongs to The Circus. Mundt is an agent of British Secret Intelligence.

Leamas This is nonsense . . .

Fiedler Mundt was not in hiding awaiting his chance to take a taxi ride to London Airport. I tell you. It is a logical deduction. He was captured and was taken prisoner by the British. And they offered him the classic alternative.

Years in an imperialist prison and the end of a promising career. Or he could become a British agent. And in return they would let him escape home. And would pay him large sums of money. My dear Leamas. I confess the thought crossed my mind. Remote and fantastic as it was. That

Mundt himself could have provided the information. I confess that I myself have been guilty of excessive reluctance in reaching such a seemingly fantastic conclusion. But I tell you, Karl Riemeck was Mundt's creature. The link between Mundt and his imperialist masters!

Leamas   I tell you you're out of your mind!

Three men enter.

Fiedler   What's the meaning of this?

Two men approach **Fiedler** *and manhandle him and pull him away. Another man returns to pull* **Leamas** *away.*

Scene Nineteen

Liz *and* **Ashe**.

Liz   Comrade?

Ashe   Comrade Gold.

Liz   How may I help you?

Ashe   Are you still working at the library?

Liz   I am.

Ashe   I don't know why some people are so down on Bayswater. You know The Party's line on religion applies equally to spiritualism of any kind.

Liz   Yes I know. What do you want?

Ashe   What do you do for your holidays?

Liz   I don't take holidays.

Ashe   Can you take leave at all?

Liz   I'm sure I can if I give enough notice. Why?

Ashe   The Party's recently had discussions with The Centre about exchanges between rank and file members in different countries. Friendly countries.

Liz I see. It sounds interesting.

Ashe Our Comrades have generously invited us to select a Branch Secretary with good experience. And a good record of stimulating mass action at street level.

Liz Which Comrades?

Ashe Your work for the Committee of One Hundred and the Campaign for Nuclear Disarmament hasn't gone unnoticed. Perhaps next time you march to Aldermaston I'll march with you?

Liz I'm sure we'd have a fascinating conversation.

Ashe Have you got a boyfriend?

Liz No. Not any more. Why?

Ashe Do you get homesick living away from your parents?

Liz No, they don't approve of me.

Ashe Are you still planning to go to Cuba?

Liz No. I changed my mind.

Ashe Good.

Ashe *passes* **Liz** *the letter.*

Liz What is it?

Ashe Comrade Gold, you sold more copies of *The Daily Worker* than any other Comrade in the Bayswater South Branch. And The Party believes you should be rewarded with a holiday.

Scene Twenty

Leamas *is alone in the dark, held prisoner. He lights a match to have a look around and he sees* **Smiley**.

Smiley The secret agent must protect himself not only from without but from within.

Though the perks of his operation may earn him a small fortune. His role may forbid him the purchase of a razor. He may be erudite. But mumble nothing but banalities. He may be an affectionate husband and father but he must in every circumstance withhold himself from those he loves most. And who love him most. And in whom he would naturally confide.

Leamas *blows out the match.*

Leamas George . . .

Smiley For him, deception is first a matter of self-defence.

Leamas George, I can't . . .

Smiley You know Alec, new men at the Circus were told, Leamas was of the old school. No degree but he's blood, guts, and cricket. And he's very strong. In a fight you must never use both hands at once. No matter whether your adversary possesses a knife, a stick, or a pistol. You must keep your left arm free and hold it across the belly. And if you can't find anything to hit with keep the hands open and the thumbs stiff.

Smiley *retreats.* **Leamas** *hears something. Guards approach.*

Leamas Come on you windy bastards.

Silence.

Come and get me can't you?

A **Guard** *enters, he is thrown as he can't see* **Leamas**.

Leamas *grabs the* **Guard**'s *hair with one hand and breaks his neck with a blow with the other.*

The **Guard** *falls to the floor, dead. The lights come on.* **Leamas** *looks at a* **Captain** *pointing a pistol at him. Another* **Guard** *appears and then finally,* **Mundt** *enters.*

Mundt *nods at the* **Captain** *pointing the pistol. The* **Captain** *approaches* **Leamas** *and strikes him with the pistol, knocking* **Leamas** *spark out.*

*The **Guard** and **Captain** haul up **Leamas** and **Mundt** places a chair for **Leamas** to sit on. The **Guard** goes out.*

Leamas Where's Fiedler?

Mundt Under arrest for conspiring to sabotage the security of the people.

Leamas And what about me?

Mundt You're a material witness. You will of course stand trial yourself later. For espionage. If necessary, murder.

Leamas He died?

Mundt Yes, the Guard you attacked is dead.

Leamas Get me a drink.

Mundt Whiskey?

Leamas Water.

*The **Guard** returns with a large bucket of water.*

Mundt Someone in London has been very clever. Did Smiley do this? Tell me. When did you last see him?

Leamas *notices* **Smiley** *enter.*

Leamas I don't remember. Years ago.

Mundt You have a very good memory. For anything that incriminates me.

Leamas I hear Smiley's doing things on seventeenth-century Germany. And I doubt very much he's coming back.

Mundt Has his wife gone off again? George Smiley certainly exceeded expectations marrying that . . . How do your American bosses say? Beautiful piece of ass.

Mundt *laughs, then focuses.*

Mundt Do you think Comrade Fielder was able to prevent me reading a copy of his report? Do you suppose I was so obtuse that I did not know what Fiedler was doing? As soon

as I read the report I knew why you had been sent.
To frame me.

Leamas My head. Oh God.

Mundt It was wonderfully well done. After you met with the homosexual Ashe, where did you go?

Leamas *looks ahead and says nothing.* **Smiley** *watches.*

Mundt *nods and the* **Captain** *and* **Guard** *pull* **Leamas** *off the chair and ties his hands behind his back. They go.*

Mundt Tell me.

Leamas *says nothing and* **Mundt** *begins to torture him by pushing his head down into the bucket of water. It is horrifying. He pulls* **Leamas** *up.*

Leamas I can't go on like this, Mundt. I'm sick. I went down to the City . . .

Mundt And after that where did you go? Why were you so keen to shake off your followers? Answer this one question and you can have something good to eat and go to bed. Tell me.

Leamas *again says nothing, and* **Mundt** *pushes his head down into the bucket of water. He pulls* **Leamas** *up.*

Mundt It is the wish of the Praesidium the case against Fiedler should be heard publicly. In front of a tribunal.

Leamas And you want my confession?

Mundt Yes.

Leamas In other words, you haven't any proof.

Mundt We shall have proof. We shall have your confession.

Mundt *pushes* **Leamas** *under the water again. He pulls* **Leamas** *up.* **Leamas** *slumps weak, half-drowned.* **Mundt** *thinks.*

Smiley You must get used to his silences. It is a mark of the confidence of the Interrogator that he does not speak unless he wishes to.

Leamas Don't leave me George.

Smiley *goes.* **Leamas** *passes out.*

Scene Twenty-One

Fiedler *and* **Leamas**.

Fiedler How are you feeling?

Leamas Where's Mundt?

Fiedler Mundt's under arrest. Our people in Copenhagen established the money you deposited there was drawn exactly one week after you paid it in. The date coincides with a two-day visit Mundt paid to Denmark.

Leamas You're mad . . .

Fiedler It's Mundt. He's the traitor.

Leamas You're mad! I told you, you're raving mad, Fiedler!

Fiedler The Tribunal meets tomorrow.

Silence.

I was worked over too. I could feel Mundt's breath in my ear. And all the time he was whispering Jew. Jew.

Leamas Did you think that thug was the single leopard who changed his spots when he switched sides after the war?

Silence.

Fiedler Mundt asked me to confess that I was in league with British spies who were plotting to murder him. Suppose Mundt were correct and he is innocent? Would you kill an innocent man?

Leamas The Circus does not regard Mundt as an innocent man.

Fiedler And suppose it was me The Circus wanted to kill? Would London do it?

Leamas It depends. It would depend on the need.

Silence.

Fiedler I've been to London. Once. Before the war. My father and mother and myself and my sister were travelling to Canada. We were refugees fleeing the Fascist persecution of Jews. We were in London for two days.

Leamas Canada's a bloody good place to sit out the war.

Fiedler We were fortunate. My extended family and friends all perished in Dachau and Buchenwald. And other places. We don't know what became of many of them.

Leamas But you came back?

Fiedler Yes. We wanted to build the new Germany. This is what the West does not understand. The Whole is more important than the Individual.

Leamas *thinks.* **Fiedler** *goes.* **Leamas** *looks at* **Smiley**.

Leamas I think I may get back home now when all this is done.

Smiley The operation, Alec.

Leamas Have you ever been in love, George?

Smiley With Ann, yes?

Leamas I never loved my wife.

Smiley But you love the girl, don't you Alec?

Leamas Is it true your wife ran off with a Swedish motor racing driver?

Smiley Now you say it his profession escapes me.

Leamas *laughs, so does* **Smiley**.

Leamas I wish you'd been there when we met at your house in Chelsea. I understand why you had to keep me at a distance. I do. For the good of the operation. To ensure its success. But I wish I'd had a chance to operate in the field with you. I remember all the talks you gave at The Circus. It was the best part of our training. The inscrutability. The glasses. It's an act, isn't George? I think I may have learned a lot from you. I like you in my head.

Smiley Becoming too friendly with colleagues isn't always advisable in this game. Even in your head.

Leamas How did you prepare it?

Smiley Prepare what, Alec?

Leamas I know you did all of this. And so does Mundt. Your fingerprints are all over this operation. And good on you. You've got your own back against that bastard at last. How did you do it?

Smiley *does not answer – instead he puts on a lawyer's robe and becomes* **Karden**.

Scene Twenty-Two

Tribunal.

Leamas *is at the back with a* **Guard**. **Mundt** *is on the other side of the room with a* **Guard**.

There are three **Tribunal Judges**, *the* **President** *of which is a woman.*

President You all know why we are here. This is a Tribunal convened expressly by the Praesidium. And it is to the Praesidium alone we are responsible. We have taken into consideration the statements in evidence made by Comrade Fiedler and Comrade Mundt. Comrade Karden

Scene Twenty-Two

will speak for Mundt. It is the duty of the Tribunal to either prove or dismiss Comrade Fiedler's charges that Comrade Mundt has betrayed The People.

Mundt's *lawyer,* **Karden**, *remains seated.* **Fiedler** *stands.*

Fiedler Bring Leamas forward.

Leamas *comes forward and stands in front of the* **Tribunal Judges**.

President Witness, what is your name?

Leamas Alec Leamas.

President What is your age?

Leamas Forty-five.

President Are you married?

Leamas No.

President But you were.

Leamas I'm not married now.

President What is your profession?

Leamas Assistant Librarian.

President Assistant Librarian?

Leamas Assistant Librarian, first class.

President You were formerly employed by British Intelligence, were you not?

Leamas That's right. Until last October.

The **President** *nods her assent for* **Fiedler** *to continue.*

Fiedler The Tribunal has read the reports of your interrogation. But I want you to tell them again what you heard about Mundt.

Leamas I've told you the office in London had not wanted Mundt to be caught.

Fiedler If Mundt had been caught, would he have been legally charged?

Leamas It depends who caught him. If the police got him they'd report it to the Home Office. And after that no power on earth could stop him being charged.

Fiedler And what if your Service had caught him?

Leamas I suppose they would either have interrogated him. And then tried to exchange him for one of our own people in prison over here. Or else they'd have given him a ticket.

Fiedler What does that mean?

Leamas Got rid of him.

Fiedler Liquidated him?

Leamas I don't know what they do. I've never been mixed up in that game.

Fiedler Might they not have tried to recruit him as their agent?

Leamas Oh, for God's sake. I was head of the Berlin Station for four years. If Mundt had been one of our people I would have known. I couldn't help knowing.

Fiedler Quite. Witness, during your activities in Berlin you became associated with Karl Riemeck. What was the nature of that association?

Leamas He was my agent. Until he was shot by Mundt's men.

Fiedler One of several spies liquidated by Comrade Mundt before they could be questioned.

Leamas You're barking up the wrong tree.

Fiedler Thank you. You may sit down.

Leamas *returns to his seat at the back of the room.*

Scene Twenty-Two 73

Fiedler Nothing could more clearly demonstrate the impartiality of Leamas than this. That he still refuses to believe that Mundt was a British agent.

Silence

Fiedler Who co-opted Karl Riemeck onto the Committee for the Protection of the People? Who proposed that Riemeck should have the privilege of access to the files of the Abteilung? Who at every stage in Riemeck's career since Mundt returned from England singled Riemeck out for posts of exceptional responsibility? I will tell you. The same man who was uniquely placed to shield him in his espionage activities. Mundt.

President Then why did Mundt liquidate Riemeck, if he was his agent?

Fiedler He had no alternative. Karl Riemeck was now under suspicion. I for one suspected him. His woman had betrayed him.

Silence.

Mundt has made fools of us all. His true loyalty has always been to the imperialists and the fascists. It is not possible to imagine a crime more terrible than this. When you come to give your judgement to the Praesidium do not shrink from recognising the full bestiality of this man's crime. For Mundt death is a judgement of mercy.

Fiedler *turns to* **Mundt** *and screams at him.*

Fiedler There is your saboteur! Terrorist! There is the man who has sold the people's right!

Silence.

Fiedler *sits down. The* **President** *of the Tribunal turns to* **Karden***, who stands.*

Karden The contention of Comrade Mundt is that Leamas is lying. That Comrade Fiedler has been drawn into a plot to disrupt the Abteilung. We do not dispute that Karl Riemeck was a British spy. But we dispute that Mundt was in league with him. Or accepted money for betraying our Party. We say there is no objective evidence for this charge. Comrade Fiedler is intoxicated by dreams of power and blinded to rational thought.

Silence.

Fortunately Comrade Mundt caused scrupulous enquiries to be made in London. He examined every small detail of the double life which Leamas led in England. I should like to put one or two questions to Mr Alec Leamas.

*The President nods her assent and **Leamas** comes forward again.*

Leamas What is it? One or two?

Karden *glances at the* **President***.*

President The witness will remain silent until he is addressed.

Leamas *looks at the* **President** *and then back at* **Karden***.*

Karden Tell me, are you a man of means?

Leamas Don't be bloody silly, you know how I was picked up.

Karden It was masterly. I may take it, then, you have no money at all?

Leamas You may.

Karden Have you friends who would lend you money?

Leamas No.

Karden Give it to you perhaps?

Leamas No.

Karden Pay your debts?

Leamas If I had I wouldn't be here now.

Karden No one at all? No kindly benefactor? Settling with creditors and that kind of thing?

Leamas No.

Karden Do you know George Smiley?

Leamas Of course I do. He used to be in The Circus.

Karden He has now left British Intelligence?

Leamas He is on a sabbatical leave.

Karden Have you ever seen him since?

Leamas No.

Karden Have you seen Smiley recently?

Leamas No.

Karden He didn't visit you in prison?

Leamas No. No one did.

Karden No one did?

Leamas You heard what I said.

Karden And before you went to prison?

Leamas No.

Karden After you left prison. The day of your release in fact. You were picked up, weren't you? By the homosexual Ashe.

Leamas Yes.

Karden After the two of you had parted, where did you go?

Leamas Probably to a pub. I don't remember.

Karden Let me help you. You went to Fleet Street eventually and caught a bus. And from there you seem to have zigzagged by bus, tube and private car. Rather inexpertly for a man of your experience. To Chelsea. Do you remember that? I can show you the report if you like?

Leamas So what?

Karden George Smiley lives in Bywater Street. Off the King's Road. Your car turned into Bywater Street and our agent reported that you were dropped at number nine. That happens to be Smiley's house.

Leamas I should think I went to the Eight Bells.

Karden By private car?

Leamas By taxi, I expect. If I have money I spend it.

Karden Why all the running about beforehand?

Leamas They were probably following the wrong man. That would be bloody typical.

Karden So you cannot imagine that Smiley would have taken any interest in you after you left The Circus?

Leamas No. God, no.

Karden Nor in your welfare after you went to prison? Nor spent money on your dependants?

Leamas No. I haven't the least idea what you're trying to say. And if you'd ever met Smiley you wouldn't ask. We're about as different as we could be.

Karden When you asked the grocer for credit, how much money did you have?

Leamas Nothing.

Karden So what had you lived on?

Leamas Bits and pieces. I'd hardly eaten anything for a week.

Karden But you were still owed money at the library?

Leamas I don't think so.

Silence.

Karden Why didn't you go and collect it? Then you wouldn't have had to ask for credit, would you, Leamas?

Leamas I forget. Probably because the library was closed on Saturday mornings.

Karden Are you sure it was closed on Saturday mornings?

Leamas No, it's just a guess.

Karden Quite. Thank you, that is all I have to ask of Comrade Fiedler's witness.

Leamas *returns to his seat.*

Karden We also have a witness.

Liz *enters accompanied by* **Guard**.

She turns to look at **Leamas** *as she makes her way to stand in front of the* **Tribunal Judges**.

Liz Alec.

President What is your name?

Leamas You bastards! Leave her alone!

Liz *turns and watches the* **Guard** *manhandle* **Leamas**.

President If he moves again, take him out. Witness, what is your name?

Liz Elizabeth Gold.

President You are a member of the British Communist Party?

Liz Yes.

President Thank you.

The **President** *nods to* **Karden** *who continues.*

Karden You have been staying in Leipzig?

Liz Yes. The Party invited me to go on an exchange.

Karden   How nice!

Liz   I've never been abroad before.

Karden   A great honour for the District Branch Secretary of Bayswater South.

Liz   Yes. I suppose so.

Karden   Elizabeth, let me say to you, the best way you can help Alec is by answering my questions truthfully. Do you understand me?

Liz   I am always grateful to The Party. And for what The Party has given me. And I know in my heart The Party is the one true movement towards peace and democracy. And I know in my heart that history tells us the victory of revolutionary socialism over fascism and capitalism is inevitable.

Karden   And you are loyal to The Party above all other demands on your attention and affection?

Liz *looks turns and looks at* **Leamas** *and then back at* **Karden**. *She nods.*

Karden   Alec Leamas was your lover, wasn't he? You were in love with him?

Liz   Yes.

Karden   You had not met him before?

Liz   We met at the library.

Karden   Have you had many lovers, Elizabeth?

Leamas   You swine . . .

Liz   Alec, don't.

President   Mr Leamas, I am warning you. This is the last time.

Silence.

Scene Twenty-Two

Karden Tell me, was Alec a Communist?

Liz No.

Karden Did he know you were a Communist?

Liz Yes. I told him.

Karden What did he say when you told him then?

Liz He laughed.

Karden He laughed? Do you know why?

Liz I think he despised The Party.

Karden When did you last see Alec Leamas?

Liz The night before he had the fight with Mr Ford.

Karden The fight? It wasn't a fight. Mr Ford never had a chance. Very unsporting!

Karden *laughs.*

Karden Tell me, where did you meet Leamas that last night?

Liz At his flat. He generally came to my flat but he'd been unwell.

Karden Why always your flat?

Liz His place was squalid. Apart from that last night he came to me and I prepared something to eat.

Karden How kind. It must have cost you a lot of money.

Liz Alec gave me money.

Karden So he did have some money?

Liz Not much. A pound. Two pounds. He couldn't pay his bills. They were all paid afterwards. After he'd gone. By a friend.

Karden Did you ever meet this friend, Elizabeth?

Liz No.

Karden Then how did you know about it?

Liz I went to where he lived. I was missing him terribly. And a neighbour told me. She knew all about it. Alec's friend had passed the time of day with her. And said so himself.

Karden I see. What other bills did this good friend pay? Do you know?

Liz No.

Karden Did Leamas ever speak of this friend? A friend with money who knew where Leamas lived?

Liz I didn't think he had any friends.

Karden How much money do you earn, Elizabeth?

Liz Six pounds a week.

Karden Have you any savings?

Liz A few pounds.

Karden How much is the rent of your flat?

Liz Fifty shillings a week.

Karden That's quite a lot, isn't it, Elizabeth? Have you paid your rent recently?

Liz No.

Karden Why not?

Liz I've got a lease. Someone bought the lease and sent it to me.

Karden Who?

Liz I don't know.

Liz *starts to weep*.

Liz I don't know who it was. Six weeks ago they sent it. A bank in the City. Blatt and Rodney, I think. Some charity had done it. A thousand pounds. I swear I don't know who.

Scene Twenty-Two   81

Karden Didn't you enquire? Or are you used to receiving anonymous gifts of a thousand pounds?

Liz *cries*.

Karden You didn't enquire because you guessed. Isn't that right? You guessed it came from Leamas. Or from Leamas' friend. Didn't you?

Liz Yes. And I heard the Grocer, Mr Ford, had got some money. A lot of money from somewhere. After Alec had gone to prison. There was a lot of talk about it. And I knew it must be Alec's friend.

Karden Tell me, Elizabeth, did anyone get in touch with you after Leamas went to prison?

Liz No.

Karden Are you sure?

Liz Yes.

Karden But your neighbour. And neighbours are very talkative people. Your neighbour says that a man called. Who was he?

Karden *suddenly shouts*.

Karden Who?

Liz A friend of Alec's.

Karden More friends? What did he want?

Liz I don't know. He asked me what Alec had told me.

Karden What else did he say?

Liz He told me to get in touch with him if . . .

Karden How?

Liz He lived in Chelsea. I was to ring him. He left a card. His name was Smiley. George Smiley.

Karden George Smiley?

Silence.

Smiley wanted to know whether Leamas had told her too much. Leamas had done the one thing British Intelligence had never expected him to do. He had taken a girl and wept on her shoulder. As Karl Riemeck did. Did he tell you he had been married? No?

Liz I could guess.

Karden It isn't true the last time you saw Alec Leamas was the night before he attacked the grocer is it?

Liz No.

Karden You wrote to him, didn't you? To tell him that you loved him.

Liz Yes, I did.

Liz *turns and looks at* **Alec**.

Karden And then you visited Leamas in prison. What did he say to you? Did he say something that meant you changed your mind and no longer wanted to go away? What did he say? Did he tell you he loved you?

Liz *breaks down in sobs and tears.* **Karden** *turns to the Tribunal.*

Karden That is the evidence of Comrade Mundt. From the moment Mr Alec Leamas returned from Berlin to London he acted a part and spun a mesh of circumstantial evidence around Comrade Mundt. The whole operation was mounted by British Intelligence in order to entice The People into liquidating the best man in the Abteilung. I am sorry that a girl whose perception is clouded by sentiment. And whose alertness is blunted by money. Should be considered by our British Comrades a suitable person for Party office. She is a fool. It is fortunate, nevertheless, that Leamas met her. This is not the first time that a revanchist plot has been uncovered through the decadence of its architects.

Karden *sits down.* **Leamas** *stands.*

Leamas Let her go.

Liz No Alec, no . . .

Leamas She knows nothing. Nothing at all. Get her out of here and send her home. I'll tell you the rest.

President She can leave the court. But she is not permitted to go home until the hearing is finished. Then we shall see.

Liz *is led from the Tribunal by a* **Guard**. *Before she goes she stops and takes one last look at* **Leamas**.

Liz I'm sorry, Alec.

He looks at her. She goes. **Fiedler** *sits with his head in his hands.*

Leamas Karden's right. It was a put-up job. When you shot Karl Riemeck at the Wall we lost our only decent agent in the East. So, I came back to London determined to pack it all in. But Control wanted me for one last job. I was to act the part of an intelligence officer gone to seed and willing to betray his country. It was to appear as if Mundt was working for The Circus. You'd kill Mundt for us.

Mundt It is you who will hang.

President I think that the Tribunal is now in a position to make its report to the Praesidium. That is unless you have anything more to say?

Something occurs to **Fiedler**, *who stands. The* **President** *nods her assent and* **Karden** *sits.*

Fiedler There's an odd thing here. Smiley must have known Mundt would check up on every part of Leamas' story. That was why Leamas lived the life. Yet afterwards British Intelligence sent money to compensate Mr Ford. Paid up his rent. And they bought the lease for the girl. Of all the extraordinary things for them to do. People of their experience. To pay a thousand pounds, to a girl. To a member of The Party. What a risk! Mundt knew what to look for. He knew the girl would provide the proof. He knew she visited Leamas in prison. Very clever I must say. He even knew about that lease. Amazing really. I mean, how could he have known to look at Miss Gold so closely. She didn't tell anyone. Perhaps Mundt can tell us how he knew?

The **President** *nods her assent. Silence.*

Mundt *hesitates as all eyes are on him. He stands.*

Mundt It was her subscription. A month ago she increased her Party contribution by ten shillings a month. I heard about it. And so I tried to establish how she could afford it. I succeeded.

President I see. I see. Comrade Mundt, you will take the confession of Mr Alec Leamas?

Mundt Yes. I will personally take the confession of Mr Alec Leamas.

Fiedler *and* **Karden** *bow.*

The Tribunal dissolves leaving only **Leamas** *and* **Smiley**. *They look at each other.*

Smiley Yes Alec?

Leamas How the hell did they know so much? I was sure ...

Smiley Of what?

Leamas I was absolutely certain I hadn't been followed to your house?

Smiley I always said it could go wrong.

Leamas Why did you wreck the operation after all that preparation?

Silence.

Smiley All cats are alike in the dark. You know that, Alec.

Smiley *won't meet* **Leamas'** *eye.*

Leamas I see . . . I . . . I see.

Smiley What is it, Alec?

The penny drops. **Leamas** *is aghast.*

Leamas You never intended to get Mundt. Did you? It was Fiedler you wanted to remove.

Scene Twenty-Three

Leamas *waits.* **Mundt** *brings* **Liz**.

Mundt Wait here with Leamas.

Mundt *goes.* **Leamas** *and* **Liz** *embrace briefly.*

Liz Why are we being released?

Leamas Because we've done our job.

Liz What do you mean we've done our job?

Leamas We've done our job!

Liz What bargain have you struck with that man?

Leamas I haven't made any bargain with that bastard.

Liz But they said you'd conspired against him with Fiedler . . .

Leamas None of it matters any more, none of it . . .

Liz But what's going to happen to Fiedler?

Leamas He'll be shot if he's lucky.

Liz If he's lucky?

Leamas But I'm sure Mundt has something else in mind. Perhaps Fiedler will make the acquaintance of Frau Guillotine.

Liz No! They wouldn't! The Party wouldn't allow that to happen!

Leamas I can see them working it out. Sitting round a fire in one of their smart bloody clubs. Smiley. Control. They knew Fiedler was too powerful for Mundt to eliminate alone. And they needed more than that. Mundt doesn't only need Fiedler out of his way. He needs a public rehabilitation. Mundt works for The Circus. He's a British spy.

Liz Mundt works for The Circus. He's a British spy.

Liz I understand now.

Liz *paces, her mind spinning*.

Leamas Mundt's London's man. He's their agent alright. They bought him when he was in England. Karl Riemeck was only ever the vessel. The conduit for Mundt. And what you're witnessing is the lousy end to a filthy lousy operation to save Mundt's skin.

Liz To save him from Fiedler. Because Fiedler suspected the truth?

Leamas And the elimination of any trace of suspicion clinging to Mundt. My job was to let Fiedler think Mundt was a British spy.

Liz And my job was to discredit you.

Silence.

Leamas They knew I was lonely. They knew you were too. You're young. You're beautiful.

Liz Am I?

Leamas They made a calculated guess that we'd become lovers. And I fell for it. I bloody fell for it.

Liz They knew I was in The Party and I'd come to Germany if they asked me to. How could they?

Leamas I even bloody helped them along when I persuaded you to wait for me. They made us kill Fiedler.

That's the truth. The Circus would rather kill a Jew than a Nazi. And let's face it so would The Party. The Party never cared about you!

Liz Don't say that, Alec!

Leamas The man at the Labour Exchange, Pitt. I knew he was in The Circus during the war. I knew I recognised Pitt from The Circus. Damn it. Damn it. I'd have killed Mundt if I could. But not now. It so happens that they need him. They need him for the safety of ordinary, crummy people like you and me. To them we're a small price to pay.

Liz You'd have killed Mundt?

Leamas Don't be so bloody naïve.

Liz You're the same. The same as all of the rest of them.

Leamas Believe me, I'm sick of all this. But I don't know what else they can do. I expect you know a thing or two about Leninism, Liz? The expediency of temporary alliances. What do you think spies are? Priests, saints and martyrs? They're a squalid procession of vain fools. Traitors. Pansies, sadists and drunkards. People who play cowboys and Indians to brighten their rotten lives. All I wanted to do was come in from the cold.

Liz All I wanted was you. From the moment I met you.

They look at each other.

Liz I always believed that people don't only act out of self-interest. But for reasons of history and politics. Maybe they still do. But I feel like a child realising it was her mother all along. Who left a shilling under her pillow for the tooth fairy.

Leamas We were used.

Liz The Party can go hang.

Silence.

And what about us?

Leamas What about us?

Liz Isn't the love we have real?

Leamas Is it?

Liz I don't care how we met.

Leamas Well perhaps I do. Perhaps I care I even allowed myself to think there was something genuine between us.

Liz There is. I love you Alec. Do you love me? I think you do. You won't say. But everything you've done. The way you hold me. And look at me. They way you're looking at me right now. I know you're every bit as in love with me as I am with you.

I want a life with you. Can I believe in you?

Mundt *enters.*

Mundt Transport has been arranged. The drive to Berlin is five hours. The Searchlight will be on the Wall at five past one. They can give you ninety seconds exactly. George Smiley will be waiting on the other side.

Leamas *nods.*

Mundt What do you want with her? You're a fool, Leamas. She's Jew trash like Fiedler.

Leamas You're not fit to clean her shoes. Now fuck off.

Mundt *laughs, shakes his head and goes.* **Leamas** *and* **Liz** *head in the opposite direction.*

Leamas *notices* **Karl Riemeck** *wheeling his bicycle towards him.* **Liz** *notices* **Leamas** *is distracted.*

Liz What is it, my darling?

Leamas *is stunned to be called her darling. He glances at* **Karl**.

Riemeck Good luck, Leamas.

Leamas *and* **Liz** *move.*

Scene Twenty-Four

Leamas *and* **Liz** *walk briskly towards the Berlin Wall.* **Smiley** *watches. Everyone watches.*

Leamas *freezes as the searchlight feels its way along the Wall and then stops in front of them.* **Leamas** *looks at his watch, glances at* **Liz** *and smiles briefly.*

Leamas Ready?

Liz *nods. They approach the Wall and the beam from the searchlight looks elsewhere, leaving them in almost complete darkness.*

Leamas *starts to climb the wall.*

Leamas Come on.

Liz Tell me. Can I believe in you?

Leamas *nods and reaches down to give* **Liz** *a hand. At that moment the searchlights converge upon them, sirens wail.*

Leamas *is nearly astride the wall now and desperately tries to pull* **Liz** *up.*

Soldiers approach from the East German side of the Wall. They kneel, take aim and shoot **Liz**. *She slumps down the wall and onto the ground. Dead.*

Leamas No!

Leamas *howls with torment and pain. Nothing else exists for him now.*

Smiley Jump, Alec! Jump man! Where's the girl?

Leamas She's gone, George.

Smiley *turns to us.*

Smiley It's said that men condemned to death are subject to sudden moments of elation.

Leamas As if, like a moth attracted to the flame, his destruction were coincidental with attainment.

Smiley   No doubt the sensation is consoling. Sustaining for a brief time.

Leamas   Followed by fear.

Smiley   And hunger.

Leamas   How could you, George?

Smiley   I never thought you'd fall in love, Alec.

The soldiers fire again. **Leamas** *spins around, glaring with rage and hurt for a moment before he slumps forward, dead himself, astride the wall.*

Smiley   A tragedy.

Smiley *looks at* **Leamas** *and then at* **Liz** *and then finally at back at us. He looks at us for as long as you think you can get away with.*

Smiley   People who play this game take risks. Alec knew that. It was a foul, foul operation. But it's paid off. And in the end that's the only rule.

Smiley *glances again at* **Leamas** *and* **Liz** *and then takes off his glasses and wipes his eyes with his handkerchief.*

He breathes on the right lens and then uses his handkerchief to clean it and the other lens.

He puts his glasses back on and bids us goodnight with an inscrutable nod.

End.

Discover. Read. Listen. Watch.

A NEW WAY TO ENGAGE WITH PLAYS

This award-winning digital library features over 3,000 playtexts, 400 audio plays, 300 hours of video and 360 scholarly books.

Playtexts published by Methuen Drama, The Arden Shakespeare, Faber & Faber, Playwrights Canada Press, Aurora Metro Books and Nick Hern Books.

Audio Plays from L.A. Theatre Works featuring classic and modern works from the oeuvres of leading American playwrights.

Video collections including films of live performances from the RSC, The Globe and The National Theatre, as well as acting masterclasses and BBC feature films and documentaries.

FIND OUT MORE:
www.dramaonlinelibrary.com • @dramaonlinelib

Methuen Drama Modern Plays

include

Bola Agbaje
Edward Albee
Ayad Akhtar
Jean Anouilh
John Arden
Peter Barnes
Sebastian Barry
Clare Barron
Alistair Beaton
Brendan Behan
Edward Bond
William Boyd
Bertolt Brecht
Howard Brenton
Amelia Bullmore
Anthony Burgess
Leo Butler
Jim Cartwright
Lolita Chakrabarti
Caryl Churchill
Lucinda Coxon
Tim Crouch
Shelagh Delaney
Ishy Din
Claire Dowie
David Edgar
David Eldridge
Dario Fo
Michael Frayn
John Godber
James Graham
David Greig
John Guare
Lauren Gunderson
Peter Handke
David Harrower
Jonathan Harvey
Robert Holman
David Ireland
Sarah Kane

Barrie Keeffe
Jasmine Lee-Jones
Anders Lustgarten
Duncan Macmillan
David Mamet
Patrick Marber
Martin McDonagh
Arthur Miller
Alistair McDowall
Tom Murphy
Phyllis Nagy
Anthony Neilson
Peter Nichols
Ben Okri
Joe Orton
Vinay Patel
Joe Penhall
Luigi Pirandello
Stephen Poliakoff
Lucy Prebble
Peter Quilter
Mark Ravenhill
Philip Ridley
Willy Russell
Jackie Sibblies Drury
Sam Shepard
Martin Sherman
Chris Shinn
Wole Soyinka
Simon Stephens
Kae Tempest
Anne Washburn
Laura Wade
Theatre Workshop
Timberlake Wertenbaker
Roy Williams
Snoo Wilson
Frances Ya-Chu Cowhig
Benjamin Zephaniah

Methuen Drama Contemporary Dramatists

include

John Arden (two volumes)
Arden & D'Arcy
Peter Barnes (three volumes)
Sebastian Barry
Mike Bartlett
Clare Barron
Brad Birch
Dermot Bolger
Edward Bond (ten volumes)
Howard Brenton (two volumes)
Leo Butler (two volumes)
Richard Cameron
Jim Cartwright
Caryl Churchill (two volumes)
Complicite
Sarah Daniels (two volumes)
Nick Darke
David Edgar (three volumes)
David Eldridge (two volumes)
Ben Elton
Per Olov Enquist
Dario Fo (two volumes)
Michael Frayn (four volumes)
John Godber (four volumes)
Paul Godfrey
James Graham (two volumes)
David Greig
John Guare
Lee Hall (two volumes)
Katori Hall
Peter Handke
Jonathan Harvey (two volumes)
Iain Heggie
Israel Horovitz
Declan Hughes
Terry Johnson (three volumes)
Sarah Kane
Barrie Keeffe
Bernard-Marie Koltès (two volumes)
Franz Xaver Kroetz
Kwame Kwei-Armah
David Lan
Bryony Lavery
Deborah Levy
Doug Lucie
Alistair MacDowall
Sabrina Mahfouz
David Mamet (six volumes)
Patrick Marber
Martin McDonagh
Duncan McLean
David Mercer (two volumes)
Anthony Minghella (two volumes)
Rory Mullarkey
Tom Murphy (six volumes)
Phyllis Nagy
Anthony Neilson (three volumes)
Peter Nichol (two volumes)
Philip Osment
Gary Owen
Louise Page
Stewart Parker (two volumes)
Joe Penhall (two volumes)
Stephen Poliakoff (three volumes)
David Rabe (two volumes)
Mark Ravenhill (three volumes)
Christina Reid
Philip Ridley (two volumes)
Willy Russell
Eric-Emmanuel Schmitt
Ntozake Shange
Sam Shepard (two volumes)
Martin Sherman (two volumes)
Christopher Shinn (two volumes)
Joshua Sobel
Wole Soyinka (two volumes)
Simon Stephens (five volumes)
Shelagh Stephenson
David Storey (three volumes)
C. P. Taylor
Sue Townsend
Judy Upton (two volumes)
Michel Vinaver (two volumes)
Arnold Wesker (two volumes)
Peter Whelan
Michael Wilcox
Roy Williams (four volumes)
David Williamson
Snoo Wilson (two volumes)
David Wood (two volumes)
Victoria Wood

Methuen Drama Student Editions

Alan Ayckbourn *Confusions* • **Mike Bartlett** *Earthquakes in London* • **Aphra Behn** *The Rover* • **Alice Birch** *Revolt. She Said. Revolt Again* • **Edward Bond** *Lear* • *Saved* • **Bertolt Brecht** *The Caucasian Chalk Circle* • *Fear and Misery in the Third Reich* • *The Good Person of Szechwan* • *Life of Galileo* • *Mother Courage and her Children* • *The Resistible Rise of Arturo Ui* • *The Threepenny Opera* • **Jon Brittain** *Rotterdam* • **Georg Büchner** *Woyzeck* • **Anton Chekhov** *The Cherry Orchard* • *The Seagull* • *Three Sisters* • *Uncle Vanya* • **Caryl Churchill** *Serious Money* • *Top Girls* • **Shelagh Delaney** *A Taste of Honey* • **Inua Ellams** *Barber Shop Chronicles* • **Euripides** *Elektra* • *Medea* • **Dario Fo** *Accidental Death of an Anarchist* • **Michael Frayn** *Copenhagen* • **John Galsworthy** *Strife* • **Nikolai Gogol** *The Government Inspector* • **Carlo Goldoni** *A Servant to Two Masters* • **James Graham** *This House* • **Tanika Gupta** *The Empress* • **Katori Hall** *The Mountaintop* • **Lorraine Hansberry** *A Raisin in the Sun* • **Robert Holman** *Across Oka* • **Henrik Ibsen** *A Doll's House* • *Ghosts* • *Hedda Gabler* • **Sarah Kane** *4.48 Psychosis* • *Blasted* • **Charlotte Keatley** *My Mother Said I Never Should* • **Dennis Kelly** *DNA* • **Bernard Kops** *Dreams of Anne Frank* • **Federico García Lorca** *Blood Wedding* • *Doña Rosita the Spinster* (bilingual edition) • *The House of Bernarda Alba* (bilingual edition) • *Yerma* (bilingual edition) • **David Mamet** *Glengarry Glen Ross* • *Oleanna* • **Patrick Marber** *Closer* • **John Marston** *The Malcontent* • **Martin McDonagh** *The Lieutenant of Inishmore* • *The Lonesome West* • *The Beauty Queen of Leenane* • *The Cripple of Inishmaan* • **Alistair McDowall** *Pomona* • **John McGrath** *The Cheviot, the Stag and the Black, Black Oil* • **Arthur Miller** *All My Sons* • *The Crucible* • *A View from the Bridge* • *Death of a Salesman* • *The Price* • *After the Fall* • *The Last Yankee* • *A Memory of Two Mondays* • *Broken Glass* • *Incident at Vichy* • *The American Clock* • *The Ride Down Mt. Morgan* • **Joe Orton** *Loot* • **Joe Penhall** *Blue/Orange* • **Luigi Pirandello** *Six Characters in Search of an Author* • **Lucy Prebble** *Enron* • **Mark Ravenhill** *Shopping and F***ing* • **Reginald Rose** *Twelve Angry Men* • **Willy Russell** *Blood Brothers* • *Educating Rita* • **Lemn Sissay** Benjamin Zephaniah's *Refugee Boy* • **Sophocles** *Antigone* • *Oedipus the King* • **Wole Soyinka** *Death and the King's Horseman* • **Simon Stephens** *Punk Rock* • *Pornography* • **Shelagh Stephenson** *The Memory of Water* • **August Strindberg** *Miss Julie* • **J. M. Synge** *The Playboy of the Western World* • **Kae Tempest** *Wasted* • **Theatre Workshop** *Oh What a Lovely War* • **Laura Wade** *Posh* • **Frank Wedekind** *Spring Awakening* • **Timberlake Wertenbaker** *Our Country's Good* • **Arnold Wesker** *The Merchant* • **Peter Whelan** *The Accrington Pals* • **Oscar Wilde** *The Importance of Being Earnest* • **Roy Williams** *Sing Yer Heart Out for the Lads* • **Tennessee Williams** *A Streetcar Named Desire* • *The Glass Menagerie* • *Cat on a Hot Tin Roof* • *Sweet Bird of Youth*

Methuen Drama World Classics
include

Jean Anouilh (two volumes)
John Arden (two volumes)
Brendan Behan
Aphra Behn
Bertolt Brecht (eight volumes)
Georg Büchner
Mikhail Bulgakov
Pedro Calderón
Karel Čapek
Peter Nichols (two volumes)
Anton Chekhov
Noël Coward (nine volumes)
Georges Feydeau (two volumes)
Eduardo De Filippo
Max Frisch (two volumes)
John Galsworthy
Nikolai Gogol (two volumes)
Maxim Gorky (two volumes)
Harley Granville Barker
(two volumes)
Victor Hugo
Henrik Ibsen (six volumes)

Alfred Jarry
Federico García Lorca
(three volumes)
Pierre Marivaux
Mustapha Matura
David Mercer
(two volumes)
Arthur Miller (six volumes)
Molière
Pierre de Musset
Joe Orton
A. W. Pinero
Luigi Pirandello
Terence Rattigan
W. Somerset Maugham
August Strindberg
(three volumes)
J. M. Synge
Ramón del Valle-Inclán
Frank Wedekind
Oscar Wilde
Tennessee Williams

Methuen Drama
Classical Greek Dramatists

Aeschylus Plays: One
(Persians, Seven Against Thebes, Suppliants,
Prometheus Bound)

Aeschylus Plays: Two
(Oresteia: Agamemnon, Libation-Bearers, Eumenides)

Aristophanes Plays: One
(Acharnians, Knights, Peace, Lysistrata)

Aristophanes Plays: Two
(Wasps, Clouds, Birds, Festival Time, Frogs)

Aristophanes & Menander: New Comedy
(Women in Power, Wealth, The Malcontent,
The Woman from Samos)

Euripides Plays: One
(Medea, The Phoenician Women, Bacchae)

Euripides Plays: Two
(Hecuba, The Women of Troy, Iphigeneia at Aulis, Cyclops)

Euripides Plays: Three
(Alkestis, Helen, Ion)

Euripides Plays: Four
(Elektra, Orestes, Iphigeneia in Tauris)

Euripides Plays: Five
(Andromache, Herakles' Children, Herakles)

Euripides Plays: Six
(Hippolytos, Suppliants, Rhesos)

Sophocles Plays: One
(Oedipus the King, Oedipus at Colonus, Antigone)

Sophocles Plays: Two
(Ajax, Women of Trachis, Electra, Philoctetes)

For a complete listing of
Methuen Drama titles, visit:
www.bloomsbury.com/drama

Follow us on Twitter and keep up to date
with our news and publications
@MethuenDrama